Praise for #goDo

Talonya proves once more how passionate, dedicated, inspiring, and determined she is. With her new book *#goDo*, she offers an excellent narrative to motivate readers to #doGood and live a life filled with purpose, by telling her own story and allowing space for us to regain faith and belief in ourselves. Through writing and goal setting, she will help you refocus your time, energy, and resources, which in turn will allow you to dig deep within your heart and connect with yourself internally.

This book will offer you guidance and the steps you need to live your best life with healthier habits for your mind, body, and spirit. With *#goDo*, you will find your identity and finally live the life you've always dreamed of; a life with purpose—YOUR purpose.

—ALEJANDRO CHABAN, *New York Times* Bestselling Author,
Founder and CEO of Yes You Can!

Talonya's *#goDo: How to Live on Purpose* is down to earth, honest, and real. It's a life guide to getting up and making your life awesome. It inspired my guts the whole way through.

—MIA MICHAELS, Emmy Award Winning Choreographer,
Star of *So You Think You Can Dance*,
Author, and "Queen Unicorn"

Wow, this is spectacular—honest, raw, insightful, refreshing, and inspiring. This book provides the reader with approachable guidance and support on their journey of self-discovery. Talonya's authenticity shines through, and her writing takes the reader by the hand and inspires them to #goDo, #doGood, and change their lives in the most incredible ways. Thank you. Talonya's style is refreshing, sharp, and draws you inside her story to give you the most authentic seat at the table. By sharing her own experiences first, you know this is not a typical approach to development.

Rather, having lived through it, Talonya traverses between student and master, and allows her life to serve as the quintessential model of what it means to be a #goDoer. The exercises and lessons shared in this book allow for any reader—who may otherwise still be searching—to find purpose.

—Siri Lindley, Author, Coach, and World Champion Triathlete

This book has it all—deeply vulnerable stories, real-life strategies that work, compelling data, and enough humor, grit, and wit to inspire just about anyone to make lasting change. I recommend this book to those looking to explore their identity, personality, goals, decision-making, and ultimately find their purpose. #goDo!

—Chase Jarvis, Photographer and Founder/CEO ofCreativeLive

Most of us coast through life, day after day, and fall into the rhythm of simply letting time pass us by. I'm guilty of it, you're guilty of it…we all are. So how do we STOP for a moment, look within and really (and honestly) assess what fulfills us and then take charge to truly EXPERIENCE that time to the fullest? Talonya's book is filled with poignant tidbits that had me wide-eyed with self-realization and provided real tools for how to take charge and live life with and on purpose.

—Oz Pearlman, Celebrity Mentalist and Host of *Oz Knows* on NBC

When it comes to finding your purpose, much of the advice out there feels lofty and disconnected. In *#goDo*, Talonya's personal, relevant, and sometimes gritty experiences beautifully bring to life her action-by-action plan to live a life with purpose. If you really want to find your purpose, read *#goDo*—then do what it says.

—Amy Porterfield, Online Business Strategist and Host of the *Online Marketing Made Easy* podcast

It warms my heart that Talonya has chosen to share her vast knowledge and experience with the world. *#goDo: How to Live on Purpose* is more than just an inspiring read; it's a how-to manual that impacts the reader square in the heart! It's not often I find a book that truly makes a difference to the reader, and this one does. This book not only gives you clear information that matters, but it also gives you the tools to implement that information in a way that is palatable. My coaching to you is *#goReadIt!*

—AARON D. KEITH, Serial Entrepreneur, Master Coach, Speaker, and Author

I've been looking for a book like this for a long time. Simply put, this book has it all. Talonya's #goDo philosophy and #doGood endgame are infectious. I'd recommend this book to those looking to find purpose as much as I would for anyone looking to reach the next level in their life.

—CAROLANN DEKKER, Chief Marketing Officer, American Council on Exercise (ACE)

This book has crystallized my love and respect for Talonya. This book is honest and raw, offering deep transparency. How she has taken control of tenuous situations and tragedy and turned her life into an example of triumph over loss is nothing short of inspiring. To then go the next step by taking those life lessons and transforming them into a guide for others to use, is confirmation of Talonya's authentic commitment to serve others. She joins an exclusive club of champions I now look up to.

—MICHAEL BURNETT, Chief Executive Officer, Success Global Media Ltd.

After personally working closely with Talonya Geary, I expected nothing less than an outstanding book. She has clearly done her homework. She recognizes how important certain principles of success are when pursuing long-term change, and backs up her selection with easy-to-understand data and research. She delivers a critical but practical step-by-step plan that connects with the reader and inspires action with each page. This book is ultimately designed for people, teams, or organizations looking to transform bright ideas into serious innovation. It is well worth reading. Now all that's left to do is #goDo!

—Joseph McClendon III, Ultimate Performance Specialist, Author, and Founder of ProSequences International

---

Talonya Geary is living proof that no matter what tragedy we face in our lives, we can emerge stronger and more determined than ever before. In *#goDo*, Talonya gives readers a brutally honest look at how she recovered from heartbreak and depression to design a life filled with purpose and fulfillment. *#goDo* is the perfect book for anyone who wants to discover their purpose, achieve their dreams, and inspire others. If you feel like it's time for you to live a bigger and better life, there's no better way to start than by reading *#goDo*!

—Loren Lahav, International Speaker, Author, and CEO of Stay True

---

All I can say is, "WOW, finally a book for me!" In *#goDo: How to Live on Purpose*, Talonya magnificently articulates the six principles of success that helped her find purpose. In sharing both the highs and lows of the achiever's journey, Talonya opens up this new world of relevance to us. We're left with the understanding that we are not alone, what we're going through is real, and there is a way forward. *#goDo* is heartfelt, funny, intelligent, and timely. For those looking for a magic pill, it doesn't exist, but you can start by reading this book.

—Richard E. Pelzer II, Founder of MEGA Personalities and Harlem2020

#goDo by Talonya Geary is a breakthrough book designed to help any of us gain clarity (and peace) with pragmatic steps that profoundly support us to live our lives on purpose. Talonya inspires—her vulnerability and raw authenticity, combined with her wicked sense of humour, transports us to walking this beautiful path with her as our new friend, to the outcomes that we create and that will serve us best. Her professional expertise and lifelong learning wisdom underpins the seemingly simple exercises that will and do embed the actions and changes you create. I strongly recommend this delightful book to people, teams, and organizations willing and wanting to develop more direct purpose and joy in their daily lives.

—LISA KAY, Leadership Facilitator
and Crew Director—Asia-Pacific, Success Resources

Talonya Geary has hit a home run with this book! Her personal and vulnerable experiences hooked me instantly, and established a mindset for challenging oneself to #goDo and #doGood. I'm motivated to #goDo with a passion to #doGood, and Talonya has given me the playbook to execute with an absolute purpose in my personal and professional life. This is a definite must read.

—CHI Y. PAK, Senior Manager, Supplier Diversity, T-Mobile

#goDo

HOW TO LIVE ON PURPOSE

TALONYA GEARY

PUBLISH
YOUR
PURPOSE
PRESS

For permission requests, write to the publisher, addressed "Attention: Permissions Coordinator," at the address below.
Publish Your Purpose Press
141 Weston Street, #155
Hartford, CT, 06141

The opinions expressed by the Author are not necessarily those held by Publish Your Purpose Press.

Ordering Information: Quantity sales and special discounts are available on quantity purchases by corporations, associations, and others. For details, contact the publisher at the address above.

Cover design by Wendy Ochoa
Typeset by Stewart A. Williams

Printed in the United States of America.
ISBN: 978-1-946384-34-8 (print)
ISBN: 978-1-946384-35-5 (ebook)

Library of Congress Control Number: 2018939934

First edition, October 2018.

The information contained within this book is strictly for informational purposes. The material may include information, products, or services by third parties. As such, the Author and Publisher do not assume responsibility or liability for any third-party material or opinions. The publisher is not responsible for websites (or their content) that are not owned by the publisher. Readers are advised to do their own due diligence when it comes to making decisions.

Publish Your Purpose Press works with authors, and aspiring authors, who have a story to tell and a brand to build. Do you have a book idea you would like us to consider publishing? Please visit PublishYourPurposePress.com for more information.

This is for you, Todd.
Your purpose in life gave me the greatest gift of all—my purpose.

#goDo

CONTENTS

#goDo

#goDo

Taking action in the face of fear, doubt, and uncertainty. Those who #goDo enjoy all of life's riches and rewards, and know that the only thing that separates them from who they dream of being is a simple decision to #goDo.

#doGood

Those who consistently #goDo soon realize that the ultimate goal of life is to live on purpose and #doGood. This is achieved when we are in service to others. Our ultimate success stories are forever written when we #doGood.

#goDo

FOREWORD

In 2010, after the end of a relationship and in need of foundation and a fresh start, I sought refuge in a spare room at my friend Talonya Geary's house.

Ironically, or not at all, it was in a part of the city called Normal Heights. When I moved in, I had just turned 30 and I was starting over. Again. And so, it was between jobs and loves, and ripped open to the uncertainty of normal life that I got to know my new roommate, Talonya.

Her house was a hub of constant communal activity. It was exactly what I needed. There were a few bedroom boarders like me. And people were always coming and going through the heavy oak Craftsman front door. Through the back door, too, with the hidden house key just about anyone in San Diego knew where to find. It was a period of go-go growth and activity and scrappy entrepreneurship and community collaboration and local politics, and we even had a few international exchange students float in and out. It was an exciting time to be in a neighborhood city that felt like a petri dish of cultural shifts and social upshots. We were grinding and grasping, and it was generous and abundant. We were also overly indulgent and undermining our strides at times with ditzy self-destruction. Trial and error, risks and rewards, surprising successes, staggering traction, kick-in-the-gut growing pains, learnings, realizations, and emotions that, maybe up until this moment, I thought I was welling up with in my bedroom all by myself.

When I'd bump into Talonya in that house, by the looks of her constant creations and comings and goings, she always seemed to be up to something. I'd shuffle out of my bedroom to find her on her second americano of the morning, journaling wildly at the dining room table. Or she'd be mapping a new business plan that she'd be talking through later on with her business coach at the

24-hour coffee shop on the corner. Some nights she was spinning records on the turntable in our living room at an afterparty she'd assembled on the mid-century mod furniture. Then, the next day she'd be out training for a triathlon or planning a charity fundraiser or a film fest or sprouting almonds to make her own nut milk. Me? I was just trying to pull myself out of sweatpants for a few hours each afternoon, but it always felt like Talonya had a dozen plates spinning while simultaneously making master plans to hoist a few more by the end of the week.

I guess all of it was part of her passage into the pages that follow here in this book.

Today, I come to understand that we were doing the work in that house. We were *going through it*, so to speak. In our respective realms of self-realization, under the same roof, we were asking lots of questions and trying to live out the answers, hot on the trail of authenticity and self-respect by way of possibility and LGBTQ party promotion. Little victories, unsustainable small-town big-game visionary ventures, and egoic leghold snare traps were the checkpoints between asking for forgiveness (never permission), telling ourselves thirtysomething stories, and saving face.

The good news is this performance was all part of the path to growing into a higher truth. And *that* is something everyone has to #goDo at some point in their lives.

I first met Talonya working with her at the magazine and media company she founded and funded from the ground up. Talonya had extraordinary ideas and moonshot imagination truly unlike anything anybody was doing or thinking at the time. And not only could she dream it up, but she was able to architect it in a way that, quite honestly, I would never believe until she managed to pull it off each time. In all the places I was riding-the-brake, up-tight, and rulesy, Talonya was always accelerating, spearheading…going and doing.

I remember we'd get in her car for a road trip to an event in

Las Vegas or L.A. and I expected the club-scene music fiend to have her jazzy, house beats bleeding out of the Bose speakers in her prized Audi A4 upon ignition. But more often than not, I'd hear *a voice* when her engine turned over. I had no idea who he was, but I would razz Talonya about it mercilessly.

"What is this?! Why are you always listening to this guy? You and your inspirational spoken word personal development CDs, you kook!"

But lucky for me, THAT is how I was introduced to Tony Robbins. (Thank you, Talonya. I am forever grateful.)

(Lucky for T, one day she slipped a homemade music mix into that car stereo—a fateful event you'll read more about later in this book.)

That guy she was always listening to in her car. That served as my initiation into the mission that I am now devoted to serving

The first of his seminars I ever attended was "Unleash the Power Within" in Long Beach, California, in the summer of 2010, by way of a ticket that Talonya graciously gifted to me.

I had little interest. She just kept telling me I had to GO. And that it was something I really must DO.

Of course, I had no idea what I was in for. *None.*

And yet, somehow it all makes sense now. Baptism by fire. Literally. And coming of age to personal power all while surrendering to the mysterious miracle that happens when we finally decide to show up for it.

And so, it is with love and deep gratitude for my compadre Talonya that I look forward with excitement to a world where everyone understands that we all have inside us a purpose of heart. Herein lies the story of how we can wake up to a life of purpose, and GO to it, and for it, and DO it. I love and admire your ways, T. Thank you for the invaluable life lessons.

—MARY BUCKHEIT
Director of Communications for Tony Robbins

"We should always know that we can do everything."
—*Jonsi*

The title of this book was inspired by a song written and performed by Jonsi, a singer and songwriter from Iceland. The lyrics in this song are still the source of inspiration in my life, and several years ago they may have saved it.

On December 1, 2008, a terrible tragedy happened in my family. My brother Todd, the eldest of the three of us, took his own life. Nothing prepares you for this type of loss. The grief of his suicide and having to say goodbye to my big brother, my first teacher and mentor, and my best friend was unbearable. I wore the grief daily, felt the pain deep down inside, and the side effects showed up each day of my life. I changed physically, emotionally, and spiritually. Soon after losing Todd, almost a year to the day he passed away, I found myself in a rather dark place, going through the motions of life, and absolutely losing it. I never thought that life would ever be the same again.

This is the first time I have told this story. This story marked a turnaround in my life, the sort of tipping point you hear about others having that leads to either their end or a new beginning. Luckily, this story tells of a new beginning for me. I'm not sure what took me so long, but sharing it with you now brings more depth and meaning to every page that follows.

In December of 2010, two years after my brother passed away, a group of my friends decided to collaborate and make a mixtape. This was just before digital playlist solution providers like Pandora and Spotify had been fully socialized. Instead, we used a compact disc to ceremoniously bond our group of friends together through music. That winter, each person agreed to contribute one song to a mix we would all use to remember our previous summer of 2010. I guess this was a creative idea that my then-wolf pack deemed worthy of a holiday gift exchange. As I often did back then, I refrained from participating because most of my energy went into either grieving or hiding my grief from the world. Regardless, this mixtape somehow ended up in my hands and one day I slipped the compact disc into my car stereo system. What happened soon after is something I will never forget. I'll get back to that in a moment.

Like most days back in the dawn of 2009, just around the one-year mark of Todd's passing, I was struggling from daily depression. I used and abused my favorite elixir—two parts vodka and one part cocaine—to help me feel alive. And as I type these words, I cannot help but feel a sadness in each of their letters. Alive? What a sad joke. My heart was heavy, and I always felt empty and alone. I was unwilling to let anyone close enough to get an honest look at just what bad shape I was in. I didn't share how I was really feeling with anyone. On the outside, and from a distance, you might have thought I was doing OK if you didn't know me. I was a diligent actress playing the lead role of a successful businesswoman, so most people assumed I had it all figured out. I had high profile successes and the awards to prove it. On the inside, though, I was grieving and in excruciating emotional pain. Each day seemed difficult to manage. I can still recall how much effort it took to put on my daily mask of happiness, pretending everything was the way it used to be before Todd passed away. I was losing control and, I can imagine, I was fooling no one. I certainly wasn't fooling Kate, who was my partner at the time. And if it weren't for her, I wouldn't be here to tell you this story. I'll also never be able to say *I'm sorry* or *thank you* to her enough for all that I put her through over those years. But I hope this book is a start.

On what I remember as one of my darkest mornings and hardest days, battling with thoughts of suicide for the first time ever in my life, Kate arrived at my house to find me naked in the bathtub, staring blankly at the ceiling. My face was without expression, my body was just there.

The room she had just walked through was in total disarray. I had completely lost control about fifteen minutes earlier, and she knew it. She knew it before she walked into that house. She had a sixth sense about my pain and my grief, having suffered a similar loss of her father just five years before. Serious intuition or divine intervention told her to get over to my house right away that morning. Kate was always there when I needed her—she had impeccable timing and great access to Infinite Intelligence that knew far more than I ever did about what was needed in any given moment.

About an hour before she arrived, I remember being slumped down in my bed. It was a Saturday morning. Like most days in San Diego are, it was both bright and sunny outside, and could be described as an overall beautiful day. As I lay in bed unable to move or think about anything other than how I was going to end this numbness, grief ran circles around me like a record playing on repeat in my mind. I could feel nothing. I wanted to feel something, so I searched and searched until I found anger and rage. In an instant, I got out of bed and quite honestly, the next thing I knew, I was naked in that bathtub staring at that ceiling. But the adjacent bedroom had been destroyed in my fit of rage.

Kate walked in to be welcomed by both. There I was lost in nothing, and there it was, a room found shattered by pain. I had thrown every bit of furniture I had the strength to move across the room. Glass picture frames that previously hung in perfect geometric shapes on the walls were smashed and thrown to the floor.

That day was a turning point for me. We both knew that I needed help, or I wasn't going to make it out of this place in good shape. We both needed things to change, and thankfully they eventually did.

But the next several months accelerated into two years riddled by countless lies, deceit, cheating, and self-destruction—hidden by life's ability to pretend you look successful on the outside. I was far from it. I was back and forth between women whose love for me, and protection of me from myself, did very little to inspire me to #goDo the right thing. I drank tequila and vodka like it was a competitive sport. I had easy access to drugs like cocaine and various opiates that made it easy for me to wake up or calm down whenever and wherever I wanted. Those were fast times, and the worst days of my life. As a highly visible person granted with both the power and responsibility of influence, I was ashamed of myself for what felt like misleading the people who loved me most and a community I proclaimed to lead and serve. That shame fueled me into overdrive, but eventually led to a massive withdrawal from all things social and all people I knew as friends and colleagues. As luck and time would have it, though, things changed. Again.

Not all days were dark and destructive. My passion for creativity saved me in countless moments, and my relentless drive for significance was both a blessing and a curse. I converted both hunger for success and a drive to leave a legacy into momentum. I knew it was going to take a miracle for me to turn my life around. Those miracles were found in every inch of humanity, culture, and art I could allow into even the smallest crevices of my mind. I turned to art, dance, and music for purpose. Did you know that music can save your life?

Ask me how I know.

Driving through the sunny city of San Diego one weekday in late 2010, I popped in that mixtape I previously mentioned, and started to listen. Why not? Oddly enough, I was in the mood for music and desperately in need of a shift in my state of mind. It was great—the most alternative mix of music that would fill even the most seasoned cold-brew-sipping hipster with a sense of music envy. This music was life! It was full of energy, gusto, attitude, and joy, all the emotions I had fully lost touch with. But it was the last song that hit me: "Go Do" by Jonsi.

Time stopped.

The external world dimmed as the light, playful, and aspirational words and energy of this song reverberated through my entire being. We can all recall a time in our lives when we're driving in our cars, the windows are down, the warm sun is beaming on our faces, and even though we are carrying a heavy heart, some song just penetrates our soul. It just gets us. This was that song. This was *that* moment. Everything around me ceased to exist as the outside world was swallowed by sound and new meaning in an instant. I was thrust into an emotional time capsule, the fate of my future wrapped in each lyric:

Go sing, too loud
Make your voice break
Sing it out
Go scream, do shout
Make an earthquake...

Jonsi tells his listeners in this song to sing and scream loud enough to cause an earthquake. If I had known how to scream in that moment, I too would have caused the earth to quake. There was an earthquake inside me, ready to break through. I was holding something back, something in, and the light I was desperately searching for started to show its promise. With every word, chord, beat, and harmony, this song was bringing me back to life.

You wish fire would die and turn colder
You wish your young could see you grow older
We should always know that we can do anything

I had a fire, an anger inside of me that was begging to be put out. I needed it to cool, so I could be set free. Through Jonsi's lyrics I could literally see my older self shaking my younger self out of this coma, telling me we could do anything—we can "tie strings to clouds," and watch new possibilities sprout from the roots of sweet surprise. We can do anything, Talonya. When our limitations give way to just letting go, we can fall safely into what is next. Just as the sun rises each day with the belief that what's next is always better, we should surrender to wonder and #goDo. *We should #goDo. Talonya, #goDo.*

The song reminded me that I had work to do: I was allowed to let go, allowed to live. In fact, I needed to. I knew I had to #goDo too.

With each verse I felt like I was being awakened by a higher power, because something more infinite was at play that day. I knew it, I could feel it, and as I type these words I recall that day like it was yesterday. By the end of the song I was filled again. I was finally ready to #goDo.

I must have listened to that song on repeat for the next two hours. It was the sonic therapy I needed. I can vividly recall the rawness of the experience's brutal honesty. As I share this story with you, I can still feel how the blood ran through my veins that day. Because of that day, that song, that moment, I can see clearly. I can feel deeply. And from those two short hours, through music, I came back to life.

Go do then became my mantra. I used to say these words to myself any time I felt myself slipping back into that space of grief and darkness. A voice inside was always there to remind me to keep going. *Talonya, just go do. Get out of bed. Take one more step. Don't be afraid. You got this. Talonya, go do.*

That's exactly what I did then and it's what I'm still doing today, ten years later in 2018. This song is one of the many reasons why I am still here today to remind you that you should always know you can do anything. As simple as it may seem, it is just as true.

Without fail, my friends, if you have a dream—a burning

desire to live a life on purpose or to serve others (because trust me, the world is filled with people who need you)—my advice will always be the same: in the face of fear, doubt and uncertainty, go and do.

#goDo

INTRODUCTION

This is your guide to #goDo, to #doGood, and to ultimately find the way to live your life of and on purpose. If you truly desire to live a life on purpose, take the principles in this book and transform them into a daily practice. I wrote this book for a few reasons. The first reason was to share my story. I knew that if my life experiences could ignite purpose in others, those past painful experiences would have served their purpose. I also wrote this book to remind you that you are not alone. You never know when your summer mixtape will show up when you need it most. Perhaps this book is your summer mixtape, a source of inspiration to influence you to celebrate a life of and on purpose. I want my words—and the deeply personal stories I am willing to share with you—to encourage you to make the decision to go after what it is you've been holding inside of you. When you finally make the commitment to #goDo, faith combines with your burning desire and the world conspires in your favor—magic starts to happen and you are the magician. Everything changes, and you start living life on purpose.

If my assumptions are true, the reason you are reading this book is because you are looking for something that is missing in your life. You may not know what it is, but you definitely know when and if it is not there. Trust me, I know that feeling. It was the same feeling that compelled me to #goDo in the first place and to search for answers that could help me feel like I was living a life *of* and *on* purpose.

Something led you to these pages. A source more powerful than us has guided you to this moment. You must believe that and you must listen to it. Not all answers will be found here, but I can assure you that the stories and words I am about to share with you will make a difference. How do I know? Because, before writing this book, I was you.

As an eternal optimist, I believe anything can happen. I am living proof of this belief and this book is a reflection of how my life has unfolded as a result.

It is my hope that this book guides you to celebrate similar success. What I found on my journey is documented in these pages. I am confident it will help get you from where you are today to where you know you want and need to be tomorrow. This book will show you how a daily practice can build discipline that spawns results you can be proud of. And it will teach you the importance of the science behind writing down your goals, journaling, and how doing both turns wishes and dreams into reality. My ultimate outcome is for you to take what you learn here, implement it into your life right away, then go on to inspire others to #goDo, #doGood, and live on purpose like you. My ultimate mission is to inspire one million people to #goDo. I need your help to #goGet there.

That is what it means to #goDo and become a #goDoer. Allow the remaining pages to guide you in a spirit of #goDoing so well that you #doGood with your life. The reason why we are all here is to find the quickest path to #doingGood—this will be one of the most impactful decisions of your life and will bring you more happiness, more success, and likely more fulfillment than any other decision you can make. Ask me how I know.

I encourage you to read this book from beginning to end. Set the intention to carve out at least 30 minutes each day to read and feed your mind and soul. If you keep your word to this intention, you will be done in just a few short days, faster than you would have thought. Upon completion, or even during the process of reading, start a practice of journaling and writing down things that strike and inspire you in these pages. Step into the process I am about to share with you and #goDo as soon as possible. You will be glad you did. Again, ask me how I know.

Take your life into your own hands—make the time to get clear, to get closer to your purpose, and to find your vision, whatever the hell it is. Doing so will take you in the opposite direction of absolutely losing it like I almost did so many years ago. Write down your vision, however big or small, and find the courage to share it with as many people as you can. Feel free to share it with me.

Get uncomfortable with this process, because that is when you know it is working.

Making the decision to finally step into a #goDo practice and lifestyle is only the beginning. This book gives you my six principles that you can follow daily, and your commitment to this practice will reveal the rest. If you finish reading this book and still feel like you cannot commit to these six principles on a daily basis, then start with and aim for one or two principles each day. As you learn and master them, add the remaining ones along the way. It is perfectly OK to take the practice and the process one day and one step at a time. In your search to #goDo and #doGood, strive for quality and give yourself the time and space to integrate each of these principles into your nervous system. I will take some time later in the book to discuss this idea of getting learning into your nervous system. Trust me, you are going to love it.

As a first step, commit to completing at least one principle each day until doing so becomes a habit, something you look forward to #goDoing each morning or before you go to sleep. Did you know that 40 percent of what we do each day comes from habits we may or may not be aware of? Let the completion of one principle each day be the beginning of one of these new habits, one you will start to enjoy. Patience supported by faith is the key to making these habits and new results last. Be kind to yourself and remember to celebrate all your efforts. When I first started this practice, I was aiming for perfection. I remember rushing through the process to cross some imaginary finish line each time I started. It was exhausting and I was on the fast track to giving up. Not a good idea. I soon learned that quality was the endgame. Celebration was victory.

With regard to this practice, let this be one of the few times you give yourself permission to enjoy the journey. Stay present with what you are experiencing and learning, as it is one of the best ways you can accelerate your success and results. I promise that if you #goDo this, eventually the daily practice will become as necessary to you as getting dressed and brushing your teeth each day. It will be the catalyst to celebrating a healthy, balanced, and purpose-driven life. It is my belief that health, balance, and purpose are nirvana. You will soon find that living on purpose is much easier than you think. It starts with your decision to #goDo.

They say that nothing of value comes without paying a price, and I couldn't agree more. However, success and accomplishment are available to anyone willing to #goDo. Consider following the six principles I am about to share with you as the minimal price you pay to get the value you are looking for in life—your purpose. Do not overthink or over complicate the process, just get started. The only decision you need to make in this moment is the decision to #goDo.

Let me leave you with these words of advice as you turn the pages and get started on the path to #goDo, #doGood, and live on purpose:

Take your life into your own hands.
Take the time to get connected to a burning desire,
    as a burning desire will lead you to your purpose.
Once you've found desire, connect with it daily—
    share it with as many people as possible.
Do not forget to enjoy the journey that is life.
This life, your life, is meant to be experienced with joy,
    presence, and faith.
Above all,
#goDo.
The world is waiting for you.

—Talonya Geary

#goDo

PART 1

#goDo

#goDo

#goDo PURPOSE

Uncover a sense of purpose in your life and you can
#goDo whatever the hell you want.
—TALONYA GEARY

I couldn't think of a better way to start this book than with those words. I believe them with my whole heart and I take daily action to show my commitment to them. My hope is that by the end of this book, hopefully even sooner, you will believe in them too. By the time you turn the last page, I hope you will have found a new sense of faith and belief in yourself, as well as a renewed commitment to the well-being of others. It is my purpose to show you how to #goDo, #doGood, and live a life on purpose. Let's get started.

MY STORY

As I sat down to write this book in 2013, I knew I had to find a way to be both vulnerable and transparent. In 2013, I was prepared to be neither. I knew I had a story to tell, a story that could serve as a lesson to teach and a gift to pass on to others. Back then, I was convinced that somehow my life could help others #goDo, #doGood, and live on purpose. So completing this book was a #goDo goal I set for myself to help me fulfill my promise to live on purpose. I am happy to say that during the times when I needed it most, this book helped. It changed everything. It guided me and gave me a place to come home to. In essence, this book became my purpose.

xThere was a time in my life when I felt like I had lost it all. I had lost direction. I had lost hope. I had lost all sense of purpose. To be alive without purpose is one of the scariest places to be.

Several years ago, I found myself in a dark and lonely place. I was drinking on a consistent basis each night after work, using alcohol as an escape from what I felt was an unbearable life. Even though drinking seemed like a perfectly and socially acceptable thing to do, I knew something was wrong and something important was missing. I couldn't feel much, but I could feel that. I was abusing prescription drugs and other substances as a way to numb myself from my life because of the lack of passion and purpose I woke up to each day. It gets worse. I started smoking. Even though I was a visible and vocal champion against smoking cigarettes, having grown up watching my mom puff out packs of Benson & Hedges, I found myself sneaking off to the backyard or taking suspiciously longs walks so I could smoke where nobody would know my secret. I remember rushing through my workout so I could get back home and smoke a cigarette. Oddly enough, I used to smoke in my workout clothes. How crazy is that? I also used to keep small bottles of perfume hidden in various coat pockets and lighters jammed in sneaky crevices of the backyard so I could strategically get away with these moments of sweet, nicotine-filled release. Looking back, these moments were far from sweet. If anything, they were empty and vapid. I feel embarrassed to even write these words.

Back then, I felt no passion. I felt shame. I felt lost and out of control. I had lost my identity and betrayed my character, as well as all who had come to believe in me. To cope with the pain, I willingly reached for any state-inducing substance that promised to momentarily numb me from the pain of living a life with zero purpose.

As I reflect back on those days, it is hard to believe I drove myself to a place where I was hiding the darkness of my life from others, trying to escape it myself. I lacked so much courage then as I lied to all the people I loved most. The worst part is how I spent each day letting myself down. That was tough. I knew I was meant for more, but I had simply lost my way. My behavior and my appearance said it all. It seemed like I was going to be unable to turn it all around.

In addition to the substances I allowed to enter my life, I had also welcomed an additional 20 pounds of unnecessary weight to find its way home on me. I looked in the mirror and did not want to recognize the person I saw. Always proud of the active life I led, I had allowed my life to shrink to stagnation as a once energy-rich life dissolved to, at best, an even keel. To make matters worse, I was financially broke. At the time, I remember having just $65 in my bank account and my rent was past due. Were it not for the generosity and grace of my sister to secretly deposit money into my account 24 hours after getting off the phone with me, I still would not have known how my rent was going to be paid that month.

It didn't stop there.

I found myself pretty much unemployed, having just lost my last bit of work. All these factors combined left me feeling insecure and paralyzed to pursue new work. My ego was crushed. My identity was in tatters. I shrunk to insignificance in my own mind and felt so small. I was in physical, emotional, and spiritual disarray, and the world around me reflected just that. It was the absolute manifestation of what was happening on the inside.

I used to ask myself: *How did I get here? How did someone like me who is educated, ambitious, extremely driven, and visibly successful to pretty much everyone around me find myself in a place where I was broke, unemployed, overweight, and miserably abusing substances to numb myself from the pain of all these things? How did I let this happen?*

Luckily, a good friend and mentor of mine flew into town to attend a seminar I was also attending. We ran into each other at the event and, to my surprise, we managed to get a date on the calendar to connect once the seminar was over. I was in bad shape, so I jumped at the chance to meet with her. I would have met with anyone who I thought could help me pull my life out of the drain it was trickling down into. I was desperate, but luckily I had not lost my persistence.

Of all the people I could have run into at that seminar, Loren was the one I needed the most. I trusted her and valued her opinion to the letter. Anyone who has the privilege of knowing Loren knows she is not afraid of anything. She is that friend who always has the courage and love for you to be honest. On more than one occasion, she has been brutally honest with me, for better or worse. And since she had shown me that kind of love and courage once before, I was counting on her that day to do it again.

As I mentioned earlier, I had lost my brother back in 2008 and allowed the incident to have negative consequences on my physical, emotional, and mental well-being. My life took quite the downturn, as I began to let everything go. I allowed the passion in my life to slip away as I stopped doing the things I loved and needed most. Loren was one of the few people to look at me and boldly give me the truth square in the eyes. I'll never forget her words: "Hey, I know you're hurting because look at you. You look like hell. You're a healthy person, Talonya, and look at you. You used to be a rockstar! You've gained all this weight and you're holding onto it to protect yourself from getting hurt. You need to knock it off! It's time to get you back. Now!"

Whoa! As a woman, those are words you hope to never hear from anyone. Hearing them from Loren, someone I dearly looked up to, helped shake me out of a living nightmare. You have to really love someone to have the courage to tell them the truth, and you have to really want to see them do better if you are willing to put yourself in a position to hurt them with that brand of truth. I'm so grateful she did.

Take note: #doGooders come in all forms, even when they show up as someone who will, for your own good, tell you when you have absolutely lost it. My simple advice is to make sure to surround yourself with these people—they have purpose and they know it. They already #goDo and #doGood. Let them lead the way. Ask me how I know.

That day we met for lunch, Loren said something to me that I'll always remember. After I went round and round trying to blame my current relationship for the problems I was experiencing in my life, Loren said, "Talonya, this relationship isn't working because you've lost your way. You have no purpose." She said, "Even the Bible says, 'Without a vision man will perish.'"

How was I so blind to have missed that?

You see, at that particular moment in time, I was looking to Loren to help me decide if I was in a relationship with the right person, when the real issue all along was that I was in the wrong relationship with myself. Loren got that right away. She clearly understood that the problem had nothing to do with the person I was dating. It was obvious to her that the problem was me. I had allowed all these challenges and obstacles in life to occupy my identity and, as a result, I had lost my true north. She was right; I had completely lost my purpose and my life was living proof of that loss.

I was unhealthy. I was financially broke. My business, romantic relationship, and friendships were all struggling, and life was making a disaster out of me. As the truth pierced my character, and shattered my fragile ego, I realized I needed to take the advice I had been preaching for years. I needed to #goDo. It was my turn. Again.

The purpose of life is to live a life of purpose.
—RICHARD LEIDER

PURPOSE: YOUR LIFE DEPENDS ON IT

As the English proverb states, "To err is human." What most people forget is the second half of the proverb, "To forgive is divine."

As humans, we are vulnerable to errors and there is not a single person alive or who has passed who has not, at some time, lost their way. However, it is what you do when you find yourself off track that makes the difference. Luckily, for more than a decade I have celebrated an ongoing practice of journaling, writing, and goal setting. I use this as a way to refocus my time, energy, and resources to ensure I can stay on track if I ever veer off. Before this practice, though, I had never given things like purpose, character, and goals much thought. When I first started journaling, it was the first introduction I ever had into the importance of finding your purpose and living on purpose. Before that, I was someone solely driven by achievement for the sake of personal success and significance. I did not understand that achievement and personal success both had to have purpose at their core if they were to provide a fulfilling life. So, why is purpose so important, anyway?

A LIFE ON PURPOSE

Living a life on purpose is the purpose of life. I know that sounds like a bunch of circular reasoning, but in my opinion, purpose carries with it the ultimate reward of living. The subtitle to this book, "how to live on purpose" is likened to the importance of living on clean air, fresh water, and healthy food. I believe that living on purpose can be a choice, it can start with a decision each day. Having a sense of purpose can provide you, regardless of your profession or financial means, with a lifetime of personal and professional benefit. I can tell you, firsthand, that when I feel a clear sense of purpose in my life, all areas of my life seem to work together in harmony. Purpose creates synergy. With purpose, I feel a sense of congruency with my health, and my career and business seem to move full steam ahead. With purpose, I wake up earlier each morning and engage in healthier daily habits for my mind, body, and spirit. With purpose, my relationships are rich and deep with connection, and I enjoy more presence in them.

But what does science have to say about purpose? Psychologists have repeatedly found that people who have a strong sense of purpose tend to enjoy better mental health, well-being, and even increased cognitive functioning.[1] OK, now that sounds good. Tell me more...

Years ago, a team of researchers from Canada and the United States surveyed nearly 3,500 adults between the ages of 32 and 84. What they found when they dug into the research was that there was a direct, positive correlation between those who felt they had a purpose in life and those who exhibited a stronger memory.[2] A sense of purpose also translated into overall better performance.

In another study of almost 7,000 teachers in China, research-ers found a link between purpose in life and resilience to stress.[3] Across the board, the study showed that the more purpose each person had in their life, the better they were able to manage their own stress. The research went on to show that each person in the study who had a sense of purpose also reported an overall better sense of health. There have even been studies that document how purpose in life leads to a more positive self-image, a decrease in delinquent behavior, and higher overall well-being.[4]

Just think about the positive effects this one thing can have on how we equip the next generation. What could you do with more purpose? What changes to your health, performance, and impact could you make simply by connecting to your purpose? The results of celebrating better health, self-image, and overall well-being compel me enough to ensure I'm putting purpose in front of me at all times.

Although we are still learning more about how the brain

1   Petersen, "Having a Sense of Purpose."

2   Ibid.

3   Fei, "Stress Management."

4   Hill, "Purpose in Life."

supports increased human performance every day, there is little argument in just how important it is to find a sense of purpose, no matter how big or small. After all, purpose helps people #doGood, right? So, if we know having a sense of purpose creates better health and well-being for others, why aren't we putting more emphasis on helping people find their purpose?

That's what I am here to #goDo.

A GENERATION ON PURPOSE

As a society, we have moved away from the idea that you graduate from college and immediately go find your place in some role at the respectable company of your parents' choosing. Times have changed. In a research study led by Deloitte in 2017, responses from those surveyed showed the millennial generation (those born between the years of 1980 to 2001) are committed to making purpose the focal point of their lives.[5] Although people of Generation X, a generation defined by its independence and need to figure things out, were some of the first to question the norms of the previous generation, millennials are arguably the first generation to make a complete break from the belief that life is all about what job you have, how much money you make, and what material objects you can buy. Millennials have adopted a new set of values centered around purpose, impact, social justice, and how they can make the world a better place. If you ask me, it's a refreshing change, and I think millennials sort of get a bad reputation for what we should be honoring as respected, needed change. I make no secret of just how much I adore this next generation of millennials, and I get joy out of knowing the future is left in their optimistic, capable hands. Generation X might be a generation of #goDoers and Generation Y (millennials) is a swell of #doGooders who are hungry to change the world.

....

5   Deloitte, "Millennial Study."

I once led a corporate training session covering the topic of communication with a group of millennials who worked at a prominent advertising agency in Manhattan. The title of the training was "Real Talk," and the goal of the day was to instruct cross-generational teams about how to communicate effectively with one another. The session included an exercise on managing your dreams in life as a way for teams to collaborate and build a unique company culture. Each participant was asked to answer a simple question: What objects or things do you want to spend your money on?

This question was confusing for millennials. *What objects? Things?* If you could see the group from my eyes, you would see a room of people metaphorically scratching their heads in confusion around the idea that money was the purpose of working, meant to be spent on things or objects, rather than experiences or #doingGood. One participant quickly raised her hand and said, "But what if we don't care about buying or acquiring things? What if we would rather buy experiences or invest in something that makes a difference?" This was remarkable to hear and was the first time I had asked that question and received such a refreshing response. That may have been the first time I realized that we are now dealing with an entirely new generation driven by something unique. This generation has an insatiable appetite for purpose. This generation likes to #goDo *and* #doGood. Is it possible that this generation is now showing *us* the way forward?

Knowing we have a generation of more than 75 million people in the United States alone who are predominantly dedicated to living a life centered around purpose, it makes sense to dive into what it actually means to have purpose. But before I move on, it's important to note that purpose and generation are not mutually exclusive. Before we ever had the chance to celebrate generational data points on purpose, the world had been illuminated by the paths of generations upon generations of #goDoers and #doGooders. Each person, generation, and evolution of thought was developed from the simple decisions of one person to #goDo. No matter who you are, what generation you were born into, or what obstacles or opportunities may be in front of you, there is no single more important decision you can make than to #goDo. From this the offspring of purpose is born: The chance to #doGood.

Purpose can be defined as the central theme or self-organizing principle of your life. Purpose serves as the chief outcome for existing, and its power is fueled by how we self-identify. It is found at our core and, when cultivated, gives us our greatest chances to grow and serve. Purpose serves the values and beliefs we are most willing to fight the hardest to uphold. If you were to close your eyes and imagine a variety of descriptive words positioned randomly around a dartboard, the bullseye would best represent purpose.[6] This purpose works as a catalyst, the dominant spark to ignite all other thoughts, decisions, and #goDo actions. What I'm about to say is important stuff. It may change your life. For some of you, it may save it.

Purpose is surrounded by a set of goals, both personal and professional, that drive a person to take action, to #goDo. These are self-assessed and influence us to invest in certain resources over others. Purpose gives us the drive and motivation we need to dedicate our time, money, and energy toward any definite goal.[7] Goals create the path of purpose, but unlike goals, purpose cannot be achieved. It can be followed, more like a journey, allowing for milestones and targets to be reached along the way.[8] To live a life of purpose, progress must be present. This journey never ends, but where there's progress, happiness and fulfillment are close by.

As we continue to dive even deeper into the topic of purpose, goals, and targets, you will start to experience a shift in your own perceptions. When you find yourself there, know that you are

6   Kashdan and McKnight, "Origins of Purpose in Life."

7   Kashdan and Ciarrochi, *Mindfulness.*

8   Kashdan and McKnight, "Origins of Purpose in Life."

exactly where you should be. This is all part of the #goDo process to get you to live on purpose.

THE FOUR KEYS TO LIVING ON PURPOSE

Below is a list of questions to keep in front of you as you pursue defining and creating your life on purpose:

Who are you?
What do you stand for?
How would you describe yourself?
How would (or do) others describe you?
What dreams are you chasing?
What makes you happy?
What positive changes are you looking to make in your life, and why?
How do you decide to say yes to an opportunity?
What makes you say no to experiences or people?

Purpose can be an ambiguous concept for some. During my research, I found four key components that, when explored on a deeper level, breathe new life into purpose to make it unique to each person: identity, personality, goals, and decision-making. When you combine these four ingredients, together they emerge as a picture of what it could look like to live on purpose. While writing this book, I took time to answer the above questions to make sure I explored the topic as granularly as possible. I found it extremely valuable to dive into each of these four key components to make sure my own purpose was in alignment with my vision. I wanted to be certain that I, too, was living on purpose. The process was eye opening. In the spirit of authenticity, I started writing this book years ago. Who I was 5, 10, and even 12 months ago marks my ongoing commitment to grow and evolve as a better version of myself. Thankfully as I transformed, so did my goals, decisions, personality, and identity. As you explore answers for yourself around the four components of purpose, you will start to equip yourself with a #goDo mindset that lays the foundation for the #doGood lifestyle you are looking to celebrate. To live a life on purpose, you have to #doGood. In order to #doGood, you must #goDo.

Read through the following four sections with the intention of reflecting on what they mean to you. Take the time to self-assess and, to get the most out of this book, push yourself to get out of your comfort zone. Doing so will give you a head start on your path to #goDo, #doGood, and live on purpose.

One: Identity

When I first moved to Manhattan in November of 2012, I felt I had reached a new chapter in my life. Living in New York was a dream come true. It was something I had wanted to do since I was a child. Being there seemed like the pinnacle of success, the peak of it all to me. At the time, I couldn't think of any bigger goal than successfully *making it* in New York. According to Alicia Keys, New York is the "concrete jungle where dreams are made of." I couldn't agree more with my girl Alicia.

However, at the time, I was heartbroken. I had recently made the painful decision to leave a relationship with someone who I loved very much, to pursue living in Manhattan. My life on purpose was in New York City, and unfortunately, the person I was dating was wholeheartedly committed to living where she lived. I was unshakable in my commitment to moving out and moving on. To this day, making the choice to pursue my purpose and move to New York was one of the hardest decisions I had to make on my journey to #goDo and #doGood. I knew it was my purpose to be in New York City, so I did just that. I am so glad I #goDid!

I bring up this story because it's relevant, it's personal, and

I cannot think of a person alive who hasn't, at some point, faced these all-or-nothing decisions. This was one of those for me, because even though New York was so important to me, this person and this relationship meant the world to me as well. Sometimes on our path to living on purpose, we're asked to make the ultimate sacrifice; that's how we write our ultimate success story. Moving to New York City, and leaving the relationship, helped me write mine. Don't get me wrong, initially the decision and changes left me feeling lost. As I got settled, I worried I was chasing one purpose but had maybe left my true purpose behind. Could this be true? Have you ever felt like that? If you have, then you know how brutal the process is. It's confusing, it's overwhelming, and it's ultimately worth it.

I found myself not knowing what to do to move on. I was so overwhelmed and confused that I decided to hire a life coach for the first time. Deep down, I knew I was chasing something bigger, and I knew I needed help to find out what it was. At first, having a life coach felt awkward and cliché, but I knew I had to do something. Thanks to the gritty lesson life had previously taught me, I knew I had to #goDo and take action to get me from where I was to where I needed to be. I needed a breakthrough.

Turns out, this coach changed my life and, for the first time, I had someone show me how to claim my identity. My identity? I didn't know I needed help with my identity! What was wrong with the identity I had before? Didn't that identity just give me enough courage to give up everything in pursuit of my purpose in New York City?

The truth is, before taking the advice given to me by my life coach to claim my identity before anyone else could define it for me, I doubt I really knew myself. I likely knew who I wanted to be or how I wanted to be perceived by others, but I doubt I had an unshakable sense of identity. How could I if I had never asked the question before? How could I know who I was if I had never taken the time to define my identity? Before learning how important identity was to purpose, I sort of thought you just existed, you made do with the hand you were dealt. Nope, not true. Turns out, you are the boss of you. You get to decide, at any moment, who you are going to be.

My mind was blown.

On my journey to claim my identity, my life coach asked me to sit down and create myself. Write it out, he said. He taught me that I had the power to form my own identity and I could do it as easily as sitting down and putting thoughts to pen and pen to paper. He instructed me to answer these questions:

Who do I want to be?
What do I want to do with my time?
Who do I spend my time with?
How much money did I make?
What do I spend my identity, time, and money on?

The best learning experience from that exercise was walking away with the awareness that you can change your identity at any time. You have the power to decide who you will be and how you will show up in this world. Because people will live and die by their identity, I have dedicated an entire chapter to creating identities in this book. We will spend more time exploring what this means, but for now, the key is understanding just how much our identities can influence whether or not we live on purpose.

Are you ready to #goDo a little exercise on identity? Let's #goDo it!

Journaling Exercise

I want you to answer the same questions I was asked by my coach many years ago. Take your time as you do, though, because claiming a new identity can take some thoughtful time. It can also be easier than you think. It starts with the decision to #goDo and write down your answers.

QUESTIONS:
Who do I want to be?
What do I want to do with my time?
Who did I spend my time with?
How much money did I make?
What do I spend my identity, time, and money on?

Two: Personality

On your journey to create an identity that supports your purpose, you gain the experience of learning about yourself and what makes up your personality. By setting the intention to take hold of your identity by creating it, you get to design your true self. Think about it: Most people have no clue who they are or what they stand for. They allow themselves to be defined by the words—or silence—of others. I have lost count of the number of times I had a belief about myself—my personality and identity—only to find out later that what others saw in me or experienced from me was the complete opposite. I remember asking my aunt this question at one of our family reunions. I was shocked to hear her tell everyone how shy I was after I had been telling people my entire life how I was a class clown growing up. Shy? Me? *Shy* is a word

I never would have used to describe myself. Just hearing her say those words influenced how I saw myself.

So, how would you describe yourself? Are you shy or gregarious? Are you generous and kind or are you reserved? Have you ever thought about the words you would use to tell others about your personality? Do you ever sit down to write about it? Have you asked others? Again, I recommend you do, or else others will do it for you, and you may not like what they say. Might as well take matters in your own hands.

Your personality and having the self-awareness of it stems from taking the time to connect with your identity. Your personality is the expression of this identity. We will spend more time on identity and the importance of it and your personality when we journey through Chapter 4: #goDo Character. For now, I want to share a unique exercise with you. Take the time to do it in an effort to understand your personality better, as well as the personalities of others.

Self-awareness is a combination of what you think about yourself, along with what others think about you. I once read that 20 percent of your self-awareness is made up of what you think about yourself. The other 80 percent is made up of what others think about you. Having said that, it's so important that your 20 percent becomes fortified to withstand the awareness from others. Both are important, but it starts with you.

#goDo: Fun Exercise

Next time you find yourself out with friends and near a stack of bar napkins, grab a napkin for each one of your friends. Pass a napkin to each person and ask them to write two things on that napkin— first, the name of the person to their right and second, three words to describe that person. Once that has been completed, ask each person to pass the napkin on to the next person to their right until the napkin arrives back into the hands of the person whose name is written on it. As a group, share what words others have used to describe you. To get even more out of this, ask people to explain why they chose to use the words they used for you. Listen and learn from what you hear. See if and how much your self-awareness matches what others have said about you.

Ask yourself if those are the same words you would have chosen. Are those words better than how you would describe yourself? Are they completely opposite of how you would have wanted to be described?

Take the feedback to heart and work on creating an identity for yourself that will serve as your guiding light. This north star will protect you from being influenced by anyone else's opinion of you. As *New York Times* bestselling author Terry Cole-Whittaker states, "What you think of me is none of my business." It holds true when you know who you are, have spent time crafting your identity, and feel your personality deep inside your nervous system. Now it's your turn to #goDo!

~~~~~~~~~~~~~~~~~~~~~~~~~

Three: Goals

The third key to living on purpose centers around one of my all-time favorite subjects: **goals**. Goals are those purpose-driven, life-fulfilling, comfort-zone-stretching dreams many of us chase daily. The path to reaching our goals is made up of the magic moments in our life that, when reached, go on to define who we become in the process. Many of us set out to chase realistic and attainable goals while others reach for the stars. Once we have a clear identity and feel free to express that through our personality, we can craft goals that support living on purpose. This purpose becomes the heart and soul that turns our burning desires into celebrated realities.

Many people struggle to understand what goals they need to work toward accomplishing. These days, we have so many options to choose from that deciding on one goal over another can be overwhelming. When I'm considering what new goals to put in front of me, I always go back to my purpose. I also consider the identity I'm committed to standing behind, as well as the ways in which I'll express these through my personality. This way of thinking allows me to fill in the space between my purpose and my goals, creating a path that seamlessly connects the two. For example, I use the words *healthy* and *balanced* to describe both my identity and personality. As a result, my goals typically reflect hitting milestones around physical health and fitness, while also living a balanced, purpose-driven life. In fact, if you were to open my journal right now, I guarantee you will find that for the past several days (and years, if you had access to those journals) my first goal typically focuses on a specific health, fitness, or nutritional outcome or result.

Goals can be tricky to many people, though. In my many years working as a business consultant, I often coached successful executives who would easily get tripped up trying to decide what goals they would commit to focusing on first. For most overachievers, there seems to be this innate need to complicate things, to focus on too many things at once. I am a master of complication, but when it comes to goals, I keep it clean and simple.

I remember working with a client who made his goals so hard to reach that it was difficult for him to feel any progress or momentum. He was always on the verge of giving up. Since his goals were so far-stretching, each day felt like a failure to him. Week after week, I had to work hard to convince him to make his goals more attainable so he could cross a finish line with success. Crossing this finish line can be just as important as the actual destination, as it shows us the rewards of keeping our word to ourselves. We need these little victories to inspire us to keep #goDoing. I remember him telling me that if he made his goals smaller, he was making his life smaller, and he didn't want to play small. I can appreciate wanting to think big, but I could not disagree with him more. We both needed him to win small so he could eventually win big.

It took us close to three months until he finally admitted he needed to break his goals down into milestones that he could reach much quicker. He admitted that he needed to feel a sense of growth and progress. I was relieved to finally hear him say this. Soon after making his goals more attainable, his acceleration was almost immediate. As someone who gets joy out of seeing others succeed, this was the ultimate #doGood payoff!

Journaling Exercise

What are your current goals? Have you thought about them lately? Chances are, the reason why you are reading this book now is because you want more out of life. You have more in you to #goGive, so there's more you want to #goGet. Am I right?

So, what are they? Are your goals attainable or are they so far-reaching you might be sabotaging your own success? Take some time to think about your identity and personality and ask yourself if your goals match that identity. What's one important goal you are currently working on achieving? If you haven't thought of one yet, take some time and explore what this goal could be.

Four: Decision-Making

In a search for purpose, you must always #goDo one thing— decide. One of my favorite quotes by Tony Robbins is, "It is in your moments of decision that your destiny is shaped." No truer words may have ever been spoken. Making thoughtful, and eventually quick, decisions is one of the most common characteristics of healthy, balanced, and purpose-driven individuals. As I reflect on all my mentors, they all #goDo one thing—they trust their gut. They make quick decisions and stick with them, knowing they can always adjust along the way. The priority is, first, to decide. They decide, then they #goDo.

I also know people, clients and some friends, who are constantly paralyzed by the thought of making decisions. It is called analysis paralysis, and it does not discriminate. Many times, this hesitation comes from staying rooted in past failure. Other times, the inability to make swift decisions comes from lack of clarity or confidence.

The reason I list decision-making as a core principle after identity, personality, and goals is because once you get these other items into focus, making a decision should become effortless. Speaking from experience, any time I have struggled with making a decision, I knew what was missing was the need to go back *home*. I knew I needed to reconnect with my purpose. I needed to spend more time getting reacquainted with my identity, personality, and current goals. I needed to see if everything still aligned. And, if things were no longer congruent, I knew I could make a new decision to course correct.

Identity. Personality. Goals. Decision-making. These are your four keys to uncovering your purpose. And purpose, well, your life depends on it.

WRITIN' IT DOWN, MAKIN' IT REAL

Later in the book, I'll provide you with a template that will show you what a daily goal-setting and writing practice looks like. But before we get too far, it is important that you take the time to fully understand each of the six components to my #goDo goal-setting guide. Part of understanding each component is taking the time to integrate this understanding by taking action. Each of these first six chapters outlines the six principles necessary to #goDo, #doGood, and live a life on purpose. If you are in a hurry to #goDo you can skip ahead, but those who want to get the most out of this practice should carefully read each chapter. I have spent an enormous amount of time researching each of these six principles to provide you with a big enough reason—the why—behind each of these key components of my daily practice. Learn and understand each if you want to get the most out of them.

Make sure you are clear on each one individually before you rush to completion. Trust me, goal setting and your #goDo is a practice. Have you ever taken yoga or pilates? I have and I painfully remember the first time I took yoga. There I was, lost in a room full of lean and mean women (and a few men with man buns) donned in their most expensive Lululemon activewear. As class started, I felt like I was the only one in the room who could not touch my toes. After a few sessions, I started to see a difference in my practice. I started to slow down and approach each stretch as if it were the most important one. I knew I needed to learn each stretch individually before I could solidly hold a pose. Progress was, in fact, perfection!

Living a life on purpose is no different. Most people want to rush into the process, thinking if they just complete the process from start to finish, they will be on their way to success. Now, I believe if you rushed to the back of this book to complete your first journal entry, from start to finish, you would see *some* success and celebrate *some* momentum eventually. However, if you took the time to understand each of the six #goDo principles—how they have helped me overcome challenges in my life, and the science behind them—you would walk away from this book well on your way to mastery. Are you interested in becoming a purpose-driven dabbler or are you in pursuit of purpose-driven mastery? Dabblers are curious or interested in a subject or result, but those in pursuit of mastery are committed to a lifelong practice. This lifelong practice to #goDo allows each one of us to go on to #doGood for others. The choice is always ours. The choice is now yours.

Below is a process I found in a book titled *The Achievement Habit: Stop Wishing, Start Doing, and Take Command of Your Life*, written by Bernard Roth. If you are looking to create new, empowering habits, I suggest getting this book. Roth created a learning experience at Stanford University entirely dedicated to helping students find their purpose in life, called *d.school*. His classes were some of the most popular at Stanford, and my guess is it's because finding purpose is something we all struggle to find. Roth's process has you ask yourself the following questions and write down your responses to each (yes, there will be multiple answers for each question) in a journal or in a notebook. If this is the first time you have attempted to answer these questions, go easy on yourself. They are not easy questions to answer, so take your time.

- Who am I?
- What do I want?
- What is my purpose?
- What do I love to do?
- What makes me happy?

HINT: As you ask each question, release yourself from the pressure of getting the answers *right*. Remove judgment from the process and put more importance on asking the question in the first place. The more you let go of judgment and get out of your head, trapped by thoughts of limiting beliefs, the easier it will be for the true you to know what the answer is. If you ask these questions repeatedly, you will likely get different responses each time. Remember, this is a practice, so commit to answering these questions today, knowing you will have the opportunity to change or update each of them tomorrow. Perfect practice makes perfect progress, and progress is perfection.

Napoleon Hill said, "There is one quality that one must possess to win, and that is definiteness of purpose, the knowledge of what one wants, and a burning desire to possess it." As you continue on this journey to #goDo, #doGood, and live on purpose, may you find your definite purpose, exactly what you want, and that burning desire to #goGet it!

Journaling Exercise

Start each day thinking about what your purpose is for living and existing. I know that's heavy, but think about it. We are all here to discover and uncover our gifts and share them with the world, so *why* are you here? If you can't think of a reason, explore these thoughts more.

What are you good at?

What lights you up?

What do you hope to accomplish in your life?

Who do you hope to impact?

I start my day by reminding myself why I am here:

I am alive to share the gifts that have been given to me with as many people as possible, with the hopes of inspiring one million people to #goDo, #doGood, and live on purpose.

YOUR TURN

Write down an ultimate purpose statement. An ultimate purpose statement is a statement that will serve as a reminder of your purpose, identity, and personality. It will serve as the "home plate" for

your goals. You can change, edit, or update the purpose statement as you continue to gain clarity around your goals. Let's get started.
Let's #goDo!

CHAPTER 2

#goDo GOALS

"We are all inventors, each sailing out on a voyage of discovery,
guided each by a private chart, of which there is no duplicate. The
world is all gates, all opportunities."
—Ralph Waldo Emerson

My mentor once told me the reason why some religions ask their followers to pray multiple times a day is to keep them constantly connected to their faith and their purpose. Sound familiar? In some religions, practitioners of the faith can pray up to five times a day. Close your eyes and imagine what your life could be like if you connected with your purpose (and an actual purpose statement) five times a day. Think about the dramatic shifts your life would make with that level of commitment.

Committing to a regular journaling and goal-setting practice is like a daily practice in faith for me. When I sit down each day to go through each of the six #goDo principles that I share with you in this book, I have faith that the process will work for me. I back this process up with the faith that if I commit a small part of my day to visualize what I want, take action, and serve others, I can truly live a life on purpose. Anyone who knows me can attest that I am a goal-setting machine. Like I shared in the previous chapter, I have maintained a regular practice of setting clear goals and pursuing my life on purpose by writing in a journal. Over the course of a decade, I have been introduced to a number of goal-setting techniques and strategies. Many of the strategies I have learned from others out there are great and they work, but I wrote this book because I was hungry for something different. These next several pages will introduce you to just that—something different.

If you are anything like me, you are looking to direct your life with a practice that works. I wrote this book because I found a practice that works for me. I have also battle tested this practice with thousands of others who I have had the privilege of working with through various coaching, consulting, and speaking engagements. The six-step system I share with you in this book is simple, yet refined. I live by the same principles and practice I am sharing with you. I invite you to get to know part two of the six principles in this chapter on goals.

Although I started a daily goal-setting and journaling practice more than 10 years ago, *my* biggest regret is that I wish someone had taught me the magic of this powerful (and ridiculously easy) tool when I was a much younger. Maybe somewhere along the way someone introduced me to the idea of setting goals, but unfortunately, it wasn't until I was well past my college years that I took this advice and practice seriously. My life now reflects the difference.

When you are young, fearless, and naïve, you inherently believe everything will work out. You feel certain life will go your way. When we are young, our optimism tends to outweigh our fear, and it typically takes life hitting us in the face to wake us up to the fact that we need a plan. We need a plan that works. Sure, you can take a stab at life and live by chance, but to ensure you get traction, build momentum, and celebrate acceleration, you need a solid strategy.

These days, my life strategy is built on intentional purpose. That purpose is made possible each day by the goals I put in front of me. Goals are the breathing mechanism to my life. As long as I am breathing, you better believe I plan to set nonstop goals. In this chapter, I will share my story and how goal setting was introduced into my life. I will also give you the history and some research on the topic to leave you with a better understanding of the purpose and function of goals. And lastly, I will give you an exercise to help you explore your goals. This second principle will hopefully transform itself into a daily practice you integrate into your daily habits. Let me start by sharing a personal story with you.

MY STORY

In 2007, I was hired to join the production team at Robbins Research International (RRI). To this day, the company has remained passionately committed to *unleashing the power within* people just like you and me. For close to four decades, RRI has been led and driven by the world's top-ranked life and business strategist, Tony Robbins. Tony used to be known for his late-night infomercials, cameo appearances in movies like *Shallow Hal,* and his unavoidable big smile and perfect teeth. As of last week, he still has those perfect pearly whites! These days, Tony means business, and his name is almost synonymous with uber success, uber wealth, and uber action! When you see this man's resume, you cannot help but ask if you might be playing life a little small.

Tony Robbins is also the author of six internationally best-selling books, including most recently New York Times #1 bestsellers *Unshakeable: Your Financial Freedom Playbook* and *MONEY Master the Game: 7 Simple Steps to Financial Freedom.* Through his audio, video, and life-training programs, he has empowered more than 50 million people from 100 countries—myself included. Tony created the #1 personal and professional development program of all time, and more than four million people (and counting) have attended his live seminars. His impressive resume doesn't stop there.

Tony is a founder or partner in more than 30 companies in various industries, ranging from technology (virtual reality) and sports (Major League Soccer) to events and hospitality, including the #1 rated resort and spa in the Fijian islands. These companies have combined annual sales of $5 billion. It gets better.

He has also been honored by Accenture as one of the "Top 50 Business Intellectuals in the World," by Harvard Business Press as one of the "Top 200 Business Gurus," and by American Express as one of the "Top Six Business Leaders in the World" to coach its entrepreneurial clients. A *Fortune* magazine cover article named Tony the "CEO Whisperer," and he has been named in the top 50 of *Worth* magazine's 100 most powerful people in global finance for two consecutive years. With a list of credits like this, it's hard to imagine how one person can #goDo so much.

As you can imagine, I was beyond thrilled to land a role on his team back in 2007. My first 30 days at Tony's organization were mind-blowing. I had never met so many positive people working under the same roof. I had also never heard of a workforce that practiced goal setting as a daily ritual. I learned early on that almost all of Tony's team members were writing regularly in a journal given to them by the company and following a specific goal-setting practice that Tony teaches to this day. In those first 30 days, I found myself asking, "Who are these people?"

This goal-setting practice wasn't just cooler talk. It was the company's walk. Goals were built into the DNA of this company, as a result its culture oozed success and fulfillment. Upon my first week of working at the company, at least four different team members approached me with a gift—a beautiful black journal that was embossed with the company's name and logo. At the time, I thought this was just the standard operating procedure for new hires. I thought it was a welcome aboard present. Thank you, I'll take it!

(For the record, I had also never met as many people who could turn cleansing and detoxifying the body into a competitive sport. More on that story in a future book!)

My first week at RRI left me feeling like I was the target of an underground program of re-gifted rejected Secret Santa gifts left behind by previously departed employees, but I later learned just how essential these journals were to keeping up with Tony's rapidly changing workflow and "top-graded" professional environment. I have to admit: I loved it and I soon learned how to fill my daily journal entries with outcomes, emotions, "massive action plans," and any other in-house aphorisms I could acquire from the team at RRI to support my tenacity to reach my goal. This placed transformed me from an overachiever constantly running into walls, into someone who found a way to get whatever the hell I wanted. Little did I know it then, but I was a budding #goDoer. I would figure this out three years later.

The more I learned about setting goals and maintaining a goal-setting practice, the more I started to celebrate success. This was the first time I felt purpose. Before this, I was someone who had an abundance of ambition but no direction. I wanted to have, be, and hold everything in life, but had no clue how to get it. With this new job and introduction to a new way of thinking and #goDoing things, my life changed in an instant. To this day, I am indebted to Tony and his team for changing my life. And it is with great honor and privilege that I now have the opportunity to share the same blessing and gift of goal setting with you.

Over the next several years, I acquired a taste for setting and achieving goals. Breaking through my goals became a sport to me. As I accelerated on my path as a #goDoer, I was introduced to different strategies and techniques for how to effectively set goals. Like I said, there are a lot of "proven" systems out there, but many of them are full of ideas and air. Buyer, beware!

I have taken the time to nip and tuck each version, only keeping what served best and what got the results needed. Trust me, there were times when one strategy would work well for me in the beginning, but after time, I grew bored of the process. It wouldn't stick. That was a sign that it did not work for me. It may not work for you either. For those of you who thrive on change, I encourage you to model the goal-setting strategies of those you admire most. Make sure you come up with a system that works for you and your lifestyle. Above all, make sure you find something—a tool, guide, resource, or a simple practice that helps you #goDo, #doGood, and live on purpose.

I hope you will find that my system works for you.

NEW YORK CITY

Remember when I told you about how I moved to New York City and it served as a sort of dream come true? Well, let me tell you what really happened.

When I first moved to New York, I arrived with wide eyes. I had no job, no income, and I moved into a fancy apartment in the West Village that I really could not afford. I landed in the concrete jungle with just enough money in the bank to get me through my first month. I did not have rent money for the following month. I remember asking myself, "Who do you think you are?"

I did not want to just live in New York City, I wanted to make it there, so living in the West Village was my idea of doing just that. What I was not prepared for, though, was just how tough New York City really is. Let me tell you, what they say is true: It is one tough city, and if you can make it there, you really can make it anywhere. New York City cares nothing about you, your story, your passion, or your belief in yourself. The city does not care what you want to do or what you are capable of doing. New York City was built by people driven to answer one primary question: What can you #goDo?

After several weeks of trying to secure work in a city where I knew very few people and had no professional network, I was coming up with zero employment opportunities. As each day passed, I started to panic. I would wake up stressed out each morning, and as soon as I could pull myself together, I set out to figure out my next move. I was at a loss until one day, a good friend suggested I speak to one of her colleagues who was involved in a number of business ventures. I gladly accepted and soon found myself on a call that changed my life.

The morning before my call, I sat down and pulled out my journal. I had started my journaling practice when I first began working at RRI, so by this point, I had solid practice. And, like every day before, I wrote that my definite goal for that day was to secure work. Of course, right? Later that day, I hung up the phone with my friend's colleague and ran (sprinted) out the door to celebrate my first consulting contract in New York City! This saved my life and served as the catalyst to my career and led to finally making it in New York City. The story doesn't end there.

INSERT HUGE EXHALE HERE.

After working for this client for a few months, I got to know just how important he would be as my life unfolded. As I got to better know this man, who later moved on to become another important mentor to me, I learned more about the millionaire and billionaire peer group he kept. More importantly, I learned about the daily practice of journaling and goal setting he maintained.

One day, I was on a call with my mentor and his team, someone on the team casually mentioned that if anyone wanted to learn how to best manage their time and goals, they should speak to my mentor. He was, after all, the person leading the entire team, along with numerous other teams that were being managed to grow several other business ventures. Once I heard the words *goal setting*, my ears perked up and I knew I had to hear more. I immediately asked for some time on his schedule. I'll never forget how purposeful he was to give me exactly an hour of his time. With a deep respect for his time and mine, he offered to give me 60 minutes the following Friday. Not a minute less, not a minute more. This was an hour I will never forget. About a week later, the two of us got on the phone, and in exactly 60 minutes, he walked me through a step-by-step goal-setting practice. He shared his process of how he approached each day to maximize time and achieve peak physical, emotional, financial, spiritual, and professional performance. What I found so unique about him was he didn't just do this goal-setting practice first thing in the morning or just right before work. He did it three times a day. Let me say that again: He religiously performed this goal-setting practice each morning before he started work, after lunch just before he dove back into business, and then one more time before he went to bed. Although he couldn't see me while we were on the phone, my mouth dropped wide open the second I heard him say that. Three times a day? I asked him why he did this practice three times a day. His reply made it all come together, which was when he shared how religions use constant prayers and meditation as way to fortify faith.

I had never heard anything like this, but it made absolute sense. Think about it. When you set a goal and then start about on your day, how long does it take you before you get thrown off course by someone else's goal? How often do you get distracted or tempted to do other things that have nothing to do with accomplishing your goals? If your life is anything like mine, then it takes approximately 90 seconds before some other influence enters the picture and threatens to take the whole train off the track. For example, when my goal is to lose a few extra pounds from the holidays, I go on a restricted diet. Fair enough, right? Well, it takes exactly one trip out of my apartment and into the world before I am tempted to go off track. That was my mentor's point. If you reconnect to your goals, not just daily, but more than once a day, your chances of sticking to them faithfully will be higher. Makes perfect sense.

My mentor later went on to influence the way I set goals, how

I write them down in my journal, and how many times a day I check in with them. I do not expect most people to be this rigid in their goal-setting practice at first, but the main lesson I learned while working with my mentor was that it is not enough to do one thing toward accomplishing your goals. You have to attack your goals from all angles. You have to find your purpose, find a way to write it down every day, say it aloud, and reconnect to it multiple times a day.

In the words of George Michael, the legend, "You gotta have faith!"

Amen.

Fast-forward to the present day. After learning, testing, adopting, and modeling the best practices from some of the world's most successful people, I finally created a process that works for me. It continues to work for me and I have fun doing it. I now teach this process to as many people as I can. I hope to build a community of one million #goDoers over the next five years. Just think about all we can #goDo with one million people committed to taking action and #doingGood.

THE RESEARCH BEHIND GOAL SETTING

I never looked at myself as a researcher, but as I started the journey into writing this book, I soon learned how important it is to understand the history of how things get to where they are today. Most times, I admittedly get too distracted to research things, but I now love to see data. Data and numbers enable me to create pictures in my mind, visual representations of how large or small an idea or result can be. These pictures help me understand just about anything at deeper levels because I get to use both sides of my brain to mix words with images and pictures with numbers. The best of both worlds! When you learn at this deep level, well, that is when it, as they say in the South, "sticks to your ribs."

On my search for the data to support the importance of goal setting, I found some fascinating statistics, beliefs, and value statements:

GOAL SETTING BY THE DATA

As you read the data and examples below, see if you can create a picture in your mind of what each of these might look like. Doing so will allow you to build influence with yourself as you imagine just how important each of these points might actually be.

Did you know...

- The first empirical studies on goal setting were performed by Cecil Alec Mace in 1935. They were done to explore how people self-achieve.
- 92% of New Year's goals fail by January 15 of that same year. Let that sink in.
- Sharing your goals with someone close to you is proven to increase the chances of you achieving your goal.
- The first step to turning the invisible into the visible is setting a goal.
- The world's most successful people agree that who you become through the process of setting goals can be more important than what you "get" by achieving your goal(s).
- Specific goals that are time-bound and measurable work best.
- In the process of achieving your goals, you will always be sacrificing something else.
- A Harvard study suggests that 83% of the US population does not have goals.
- Most personal development gurus agree that goals should be carried around with you all the time.
- I have been known to bring a journal and pen with me to dinner. #truestory

KEEPING A JOURNAL

I find myself having to make the case for writing down your goals and seeing them in your handwriting. I have lost count of how many conversations I have led, hoping to inspire others to start keeping a journal. Some people tell me they don't need to keep a journal because they establish their goals in their mind, or they can visualize what their goals are at any given time. They tell me this is enough for them to get success, but I'm not buying it. I believe that getting goals out of your head and onto paper creates a world of new possibilities. The moment the goal is out of your head and displayed on a piece of paper, the resources needed to help that goal actualize are unlocked. A path to connect resources to ideas is created in an instant. If that isn't enough to influence you to start writing down your goals, then consider the list below. This list continues to make a compelling case as to why having goals is not enough. You also need to write them down.

- Personal development professionals agree that goals should be written down to increase their efficacy.
- Only 3 out of every 100 adults write down their goals on paper.
- 14% of people have a goal plan in mind, but they remain unwritten.
- People with written goals are 50% more likely to achieve their goals than people who do not write down their goals.
- Goals you keep in your mind are more likely to be jumbled and confused with the other 1,500 thoughts per minute the average human being experiences.
- The act of writing down a goal serves as a more powerful motivator than thinking or saying a goal.
- Writing down goals forces us to avoid being too vague. Writing creates clarity. Clarity leads to focus. And focus delivers results.

Although the above is just the tip of the iceberg, I hope these points help you begin to see the importance of writing down your goals and maintaining a daily journaling practice. I hope the list above is enough to compel you to get started today.

Are you excited to #goDo? What are you waiting for? New Year's Eve?

THE GOAL OF A NEW YEAR

One study done by Statistic Brain, which decidedly analyzed New Year's goals, conveys a very similar fact to various other studies, which is that very few people achieve their goals. The study astonishingly claims that just 8 percent of people achieve their New Year's goals.[9] Are you picking up what I am putting down? This means that a resounding 92 percent of people who set out to achieve a goal end up in failure. That's just sad and unnecessary to me. The study also claims that 45 percent of Americans usually make goals, 17 percent of them infrequently make goals, and 38 percent never make goals.[10]

Another interesting measure about the study from Statistic Brain showed that 75 percent of people made it through the first week with success; 71 percent of people made it past two weeks; 64 percent of people made it past one month; and 46 percent of people made it past six months before they threw in the proverbial towel.[11]

Where do you fit into these percentages?

I find it fascinating that 25 percent of people do not even make it through the first week of sticking to their New Year's resolution, and it's disappointing that only 8 percent actually achieved their goals. To put this into perspective, there are about 300 million people in America, and 62 percent of them either usually or

---

9   Wanderlust Worker, "Harvard."

10   Ibid.

11   Ibid.

infrequently make New Year's resolutions. We're talking about 186 million people who actually have a shot at living on purpose. If 186 million people in America are setting goals, that means 171.12 million are giving up on their goals. There should be no surprise as to why so many Americans are so unhappy. Are you starting to see how important it is to set and write down your goals?

As dismal as this sounds, teaching others how to #goDo and set goals the right way is exactly where I saw my opportunity to #doGood and make a difference. I knew that if I could create a plan that was easy to follow, one that had results baked into it, I was certain I could change that number. If, through this book, I am able to affect 1 percent of those who are giving up on their purpose, dreams, and goals, then I will have lived a life that successfully impacted and changed the lives of almost two million people!

Are you in? Let's #goDo it together.

> *"A goal properly set is halfway reached."*
> —Zig Ziglar

WHAT GOALS?

So, how do you know what goals to focus on? The previous chapter was purely dedicated to one of the most important subjects around personal and professional fulfillment and development: Purpose. The chapter gave multiple avenues to connect or reconnect to your purpose. However, many people become overwhelmed by what goals to focus on and why. As a result, I have put the following together to help aid you in deciding what goals to focus on and why. Remember, though, you can always change what goal you decide to pursue and you can always edit or expand the goals along the way. The ultimate outcome is to celebrate who you will become in the process, more than the goal itself. So, as you decide what goals will support living on purpose, also take into consideration the person you would like to become. Goals are great. Loving who you are each day as you chase those goals? Priceless.

One of my goals once was to lose 20 pounds; however, for years I kept failing. Year after year, journal entry after journal entry, I was coming up short. My focus during this time was always on "My goal is to lose 20 pounds." Well, guess what happens when you lose something? You tend to find it again. Sound familiar?

As I course corrected, I shifted my focus from the actual loss (or release) of 20 pounds toward a newly articulated goal that had a new identity baked into it. This new goal and identity helped me to #goDo:

"My goal is to become a constantly disciplined and consistent person who keeps her word to living as a health and fitness enthusiast who easily releases all unnecessary weight that is holding me back from living a life on purpose."

Can you see and feel the difference? To this day, advancing my health and fitness remains one of my top three goals at any given time. I attach certain targets (we will get to targets in Chapter 6) to build momentum and milestones into the process, but the goal is infinitely more inspiring than "losing 20 pounds."

I've worked with personal and professional coaches for years and they all have one thing in common: goals. While working with one particular business coach years ago, I learned to start a goal-setting practice with just three simple goals in three simple categories. Our outcome was to focus on only three areas of life that I felt had the biggest impact on all other categories of one's life. We agreed to keep it short and simple. To get started, we focused on a personal goal, a career goal, and a financial goal. Together, we believed that this triad of goals could influence me to #goDo anything! I still agree.

To this day, I am always pursuing three goals at any given time. Once I achieve one of these three, I replace it with a new goal and the cycle continues. Your goals can range from personal to financial, and below is a guide to help you get started on what goals you should focus on first. I have provided you with a sample set of three goals that you can use as a model.

Health & Fitness Goal

Decrease my body fat by 10 percent by the end of the year, and become a health and fitness enthusiast who maintains a target weight.

Career/Mission/Purpose Goal

Create, launch, and grow a business that inspires people and creates unforgettable learning experiences while generating $10 million in annual revenue.

Financial Goal

Achieve financial security by December 31, which means having at least 12 months of expenses in savings and no debt.

Journaling Exercise

YOUR TURN

Write down three important goals you hope to achieve by the end of this year or by another date that makes the most sense. The below categories are just suggestions to help you get focused:

1. Personal/Relationship or Health/Fitness Goal
2. Career/Business/Mission Goal
3. Financial Goal
   This year, consider these questions:

Where do I see myself now?
Where do I see myself going?
What do I want to #goDo to get there?
Who would I like to become in the process?

Before setting specific goals, it helps to take inventory on your life. Our lives generally consist of eight unique categories that, when combined, create a life on purpose. Have you ever thought about giving yourself a score around how you are doing in life? Maybe you have done this process before in some other form, but it is important and a real gut check to self-assess how well you are #goDoing in each of the eight areas.

Let's try it! On a scale of 1 to 10, with 1 being totally dissatisfied and 10 being extremely fulfilled, score your current performance around each of these categories of life:

1. **HEALTH & FITNESS**
    Score: _____

Why did you give yourself this score?
....

2. **MONEY & FINANCES**
    Score: _____

Why did you give yourself this score?
....

3. **CAREER/BUSINESS/MISSION**
    Score: _____

Why did you give yourself this score?
....

4. RECREATION & FREE TIME
Score: _____

Why did you give yourself this score?
....

5. LOVE & RELATIONSHIPS
Score: _____

Why did you give yourself this score?
....

6. TIME
Score: _____

Why did you give yourself this score?
....

7. FAMILY & FRIENDS
Score: _____

Why did you give yourself this score?
....

8. PERSONAL GROWTH
Score: _____

Why did you give yourself this score?
....

~~~~~~

SOMETHING TO THINK ABOUT

Where can you build a taller and stronger building to make the landscape of your life even greater? Most of us already have areas of our lives that are going well and we are experiencing success, growth, and fulfillment. But, there are always other areas of our lives where we need to dedicate more time, focus, and energy to grow. Unfortunately, many of us tend to fall into the trap of staying comfortable. We continue to grow in the areas of our lives where we are strongest, rather than shifting our efforts and using our strengths to focus on the areas of our lives where we are weakest and need the most attention. Keep those areas in mind as you move on to writing out your goals for this year. Get ready to #goDo something unforgettable!

Journaling Exercise

Remember that by writing down your goals, dreams, and desires you are able to remind yourself of what's most important to you. You can hold yourself accountable to your desires. And you can manifest your dreams into a reality you can celebrate with others. This is the path to living on purpose.

Write down what success you would like to experience in each of these eight areas of your life. I am going to assume you thoroughly read the first chapter and have hopefully taken some time to visualize what living a life of and on purpose looks like for you. It's now time to pull this vision from your mind and put pen to paper. Continue to keep purpose in front of you. Doing so will get you to #goDo, #doGood, and live on purpose much sooner than you realize.

HEALTH & FITNESS
How do I want to see my health and fitness improve this year?

MONEY & FINANCES
How do I want to see my money and finances grow this year?

CAREER/BUSINESS/MISSION
Where do I want to take my business, my career, or my mission this year?

RECREATION OR FREE TIME
What vacations or experiences do I want to celebrate? What fun and new activities do I want to include in my free time?

LOVE & RELATIONSHIPS
What commitments do I want to make to my partner? Or what type of person do I want to attract to share my life with this year?

TIME
How do I want to manage my time? What would I like to eliminate to create more time for myself to enjoy other things this year? How can I be more efficient with my time?

FAMILY & FRIENDS
How do I want to spend time with my friends and family this year? How can I improve the quality of my relationships?

PERSONAL GROWTH
How do I want to grow this year? What changes do I want to see in my personal growth and development this year?

~~~~~~

Now that you have an idea of where you are and where you want to be, let's #goDo and make this your most focused, productive, and unforgettable year to date.

Let's #goDo more...

Scan Me

#goDo PREDICTIONS

"The best way to predict your future is to create it."
—ABRAHAM LINCOLN

I love this quote by Abraham Lincoln. The first time I saw it, it was displayed on the wall at a business where I used to work. The irony is this same company that proudly displayed this quote on its hallway was a company I resented working at due to what I felt was its sheer lack of creativity. I could not think of a less creative atmosphere to work in than this place. It had a boilerplate style of doing things, where everything that could have spawned creativity was masked by something that had been tested, tried, and true. It was the quintessential "this is how we've always done it" organization. Yes, it was a smart way of doing business if you wanted to grow exponentially, but for a born creator like myself, it was a job equivalent to sleepwalking. Sure, some people do it, but it doesn't mean it's good for their health.

I remember passing by that picture and laughing at it every time I walked upstairs to talk to someone in sales or accounting. Creativity? Are you kidding me? This place had about as much room for creativity as the Marines. Regardless of what I felt was the company's lack of innovation, that picture on the wall and the sentiment behind the quote has remained with me ever since. You see, everything has a purpose.

CREATION: A HOW-TO

How does one create a future? What does that really mean? It seems too optimistic and makes me believe in a world where I can just wake up, close my eyes, and my dream world appears. *Voila!* Well, no. That's not quite how it works, but it is easier than most people think.

I have looked into the science of creativity to see how it works and how it can be attached to one's purpose. Luckily, we are living in times where an abundance of research has been conducted about the brain that shows the links between science and creativity. The book *Think and Grow Rich* by Napoleon Hill reminds us that, in fact, all things start in the grey matter of our minds. Anything you and I experience as real life started with an idea.

Creativity represents a world where anything is possible, and when creativity is fueled by a purpose—a burning desire to create something from nothing—it becomes unstoppable. As I wrote this book, and after following a hunch to practice what it would be like to predict my fate before it happens on a daily basis, I knew I had to spend time on the subject. Back when I was designing my own daily practice, I spent time exploring the question of what would happen if I spent time each day writing down what I thought would happen that day, before it happened. I became so fascinated by this possibility that I began to test what would happen if I tried to get ahead of the day before it happened. Could I predict my own future?

Let me tell you that a good trick to #goDo and #doGood is to believe you can predict what you will #goDo. Spending time each day thinking about what I would like to see, feel, hear, and know was going to happen each day actually had an influence on what actually *did* happen each day. Let me explain.

PAST, PRESENT...FUTURE?

Let's start with the past. Most people tend to live in the past and get absorbed by the idea that what has happened to them in their past has already determined what will happen to them in their future. A lot of people believe their past can be single-handedly blamed for all their present problems. They believe their past equals their future. Many of these same people believe their present challenges cannot be changed because of past circumstances. It's just not true.

Unfortunately, the past haunts people because, for many of them, it represents pain, failure, and regret. These supposed failures prevent them from believing things can change, things will change, they must change. We all carry with us a mental filing cabinet full of stories about people or experiences that have hurt us, the jobs we were never selected for, the relationships that took a turn for the worse, and the broken bones of poor decisions. The past is a place where we have left our innocence, given away our curiosity, and somehow let our insatiable hunger for adventure, risk, and reward wane. The past will forever be a magical place for some of us and a graveyard of pain for others. Sure, they are not the same for everyone, but our past experiences can have a significant hold on us when and if we let them. Sometimes the past creates a painful connection and other times it serves as all the evidence we need about what great things are still possible. It is either a warning or an example.

Before we knew any better, people who were simply nostalgic used to be misdiagnosed as depressed. Many a self-help guru will dissuade you from living in the past because it can get in the way of your progress or your ability to create a different or better future. I read an article once that looked at people who had gone away for war and how their simple nostalgia typecast them as someone who was caught up in their memories.[12] People used to believe that a nostalgic person was mentally incapable of enjoying the present moment. It was actually viewed as an illness and a burden.

According to John Tierney of the *New York Times,* in the 17th century a Swiss physician deemed soldiers mentally and physically ill due to their deep desire to come home.[13] However, since more research has been conducted, quite the opposite has been proven. In fact, we can now show that nostalgia, which is really celebrating past positive experiences, actually works well to counteract depression.

Looking for a way to deal with anxiety or loneliness? Why not think back to a time in your life when you were celebrating? These acts of reminiscing about past successes can actually help improve your emotional well-being as well as how you interact with others. It turns out that when people speak fondly and thoughtfully about their past, they have a tendency to become just as hopeful about their future. So, contrary to what some gurus say, go ahead and revisit your past. Just make sure you're recalling the good memories, because they can serve as positive reminders that you can look forward to what's to come.

How are you using the past? Is it helping you or hurting you? Are you using the past as a warning or an example? Where your focus goes, your future will grow. Knowing that, you might as well make sure you are focusing on the moments of your life that bring you the most joy and celebration.

PRESENTS IN PRESENCE

The present moment can be just as brutal or euphoric as the past. Imagine a time in your life when something dramatic happened: You fought with your spouse or significant other, your boss or

12   Martin, "Science."
13   Ibid.

business partner dropped a truth bomb on you that meant business could or would not go on as usual, or you caught a horrible seasonal flu. When these things happen, they become all we can think of as they get in the way of everything else we try to do. These things trip up our daily purpose, our goals, and get in the way of what we might have wanted to see out of each day. It seems that, unless things are running smoothly in our lives, we can easily get fixated on what happened in the past or what we are trying to force in the future. Ask me how I know.

Have you ever been in love? That is a present moment we never want to end. I remember falling in love and getting obsessed with the feeling of euphoria you get from all that oxytocin flowing through the brain. When you have butterflies in your stomach from meeting someone new, your dopamine levels skyrocket. Your brain releases dopamine, which gives you an extra high just by seeing your new love. Brain research has shown that this surge in chemicals gives you an intense craving to be around this person. It creates an addiction, which is why you have the feeling that you cannot live without the person. A neurotrophin accompanies all this euphoria and increases your emotional dependency. Neurotrophins are a family of proteins that send out signals to cells. These signals tell the cells what to do, like grow or form in other unique ways.

Have you ever been in a codependent relationship, or felt like you were in one? Well, here is a great explanation around the role neurotrophins play in the matter. As distance is formed between you and the person you're in a relationship with, your serotonin levels drop, leaving you with both an emotional and a physical need to be near this person again to raise your serotonin levels. Serotonin controls your mood, and with an increase in serotonin, you'll experience an improved mood. As your levels drop, so does your mood. All this brain activity makes a chemical cocktail that explains why lovestruck couples can be so infatuated with each other. Their levels may just be too high or too low. Studies show that the chemical concentrations brewing inside the brains of newly minted lovebirds are similar to those who suffer from Obsessive Compulsive Disorder. A sort of intense response or pattern is created as the individuals' experiences spikes their levels of brain proteins. If you can imagine, a similar obsession or addiction can be triggered in relation to the present moment. It's just as debilitating as an addiction to the past. But what about the future?

BACK TO THE FUTURE

In the wake of those living in the past and those enjoying the present moment, there are others who stay blissfully infatuated with the future. Some are constantly worried about whether things will go wrong or right, while others live detached from the surprise of what may come. It is this fear of the unknown we grow to love and hate. It is the emotional equivalent to the Wild Wild West of time intoxication. There is a way to harness this fear or excitement and turn it into one of your greatest assets to #goDo and #doGood, and I use it daily to help me live on purpose.

I make it part of my daily practice to visualize what my future will look and feel like. I enjoy it and find it powerful enough to dedicate time in my daily goal-setting practice to live there. I call this my prediction or *Daily Fortune Cookie,* a simple and promising fortune I get to write. There are no surprises when I crack it open.

Have you ever opened up a fortune cookie only to find that the fortune was a total bust? What a letdown! All that time spent twirling those fortune cookies on the table, forcing yourself to get energetically connected to one of them in a date with destiny. Maybe I'm the only one who does that. I can put a lot of energy into a fortune cookie. That is a game I take seriously.

Imagine if you could have written the fortune you are about

to crack open. What would that be like? That's what I am here to show you, because I have always considered myself someone who looks more toward the future. I love to research trends to help me predict what I believe will happen next. I have built businesses off the predictions of human behavior and have advised clients based on the future pacing skills I have developed over the years. My favorite books and thought leaders share trends based on people, the economy, and changes in technology. Each of these books promises to show you where the shifts in an era are likely to happen. There is only one past; there can only be one present; but there are many potential futures. OK, that's exciting!

In 2013, I met a futurist named David Houle. For the record, I had zero clue what a futurist was until I met one for the first time. They are social scientists. These scientists, or futurologists, predict future human behavior and social development by reviewing data from past human behavior and development.

David is an author, futurist, thinker, and great public speaker. He spent more than 20 years in media and entertainment; has worked at NBC and CBS; and was part of the senior executive team that created and launched MTV, Nickelodeon, VH1, and CNN Headline News. I hired David to speak at a conference I was organizing and, during the beginning of our relationship, he sent me a copy of the book he had just published, *Entering the Shift Age*. I was taken by the book's promise to tell you what to expect for the next several decades. As someone who's made a serious hobby of predicting what's next, this book hit the spot.

Here's one of my favorite quotes from the book that provides an accurate look into what it means to be living in the Shift Age: "While ages and stages of history often overlap and blend into each other, there are simple conceptual characteristics to every age. Tools defined the Agricultural Age. Machines defined the Industrial Age. Technology defined the Information Age. Consciousness will define the Shift Age."

What is fascinating about David's book is its relentless commitment to predicting what is going to happen next in technology, the economy, politics, the environment, and even humanity. The book takes a historical look at the past, plotting major generational shifts and technological advances onto a timeline. Like other futurists, the author then calculates the patterns that exist within and throughout the data to serve as markers. He is methodical in his approach to pinpointing exact times in our social evolution where we collectively shift. I loved how David boldly put himself out there to tell you, not just what to prepare for negatively, but to also show you how to positively prepare yourself for advantage, for opportunity, and for all things that could shift in your favor.

We now live in the Shift Age, a time of transformation that will be regarded by future historians as one of the most significant periods in human history. The Shift Age is one of those changes in direction or times when much of humanity will change how we live, how we think, how we interact with each other, and what we do.

I still think about this book often and reference key points from it on an ongoing basis. As we discuss predicting our futures here, I would recommend *Entering the Shift Age* to anyone who wants to make predictions in their own life based on the strengths we are experiencing collectively.

The book also helped me to become a futurist in my own world. Based on taking a glance behind me, I could see where my own shifts might possibly occur. Some of these shifts were not the best experiences, sometimes leading me down paths I may have preferred to miss entirely. Like the time I thought it was a great idea to start dressing like a hippie, and considered dropping out of college to pursue a career as a professional snowboarder. Shut the front door, right? Yes, I'll never forget going home that Christmas to gather my family around the dinner table and declare my big plans to leave college and all the scholarships I had earned. You can imagine my mom's excitement, after all that she and my step-father had sacrificed to support my music ambitions over the past decade. They were, let me just say, less than amused with this idea. You cannot see me, but I am rolling my eyes as I type this.

Luckily, my parents were also practicing futurists who knew if I dropped out of school for a year, the chances of me going back would have diminished dramatically. I guess you don't need to be a futurist to know this. Fortunately, they talked me out of this decision.

I have experienced other shifts in my life that changed its entire course in ways I never would have imagined. One of the stories I always share is how making the decision to start working with Tony Robbins back in 2007 changed my life. At the time, I had no clue who Tony was. I was working for a large production company that produced a variety of large-scale creative live events. I loved the work, but I did not love my boss. Can I get an amen? I was miserable with this guy. All he could think about was how much money he was going to make off of his clients. He cared very little about any sort of culture of happiness of the individuals who worked so hard to make that money for him. My assumption is that his only purpose in life revolved around making money.

I started job searching because I felt morally bankrupt each day I walked into the office and remained complicit on his team. I know many of you know that feeling, and I feel for you. All I can say is believe in yourself, have faith, and get the hell out of there...fast.

On my job search, I ran across the job posting to work with Tony Robbins and, I'll admit, the only thing that convinced me to pursue the opportunity was when I visited the corporate web-site and noticed how many big events Tony spoke at around the world—Fiji, London, Scotland. Traveling the world like this was a dream come true for me, so my eyes lit up like Canadian dollars just thinking about how this career move might add to my pass-port stamp collection. "I'll do it, Mr. Robbins! Count me in!"

The decision did just that—it changed my life. I went from having an abundance of ambition and nowhere to effectively place it, to living a healthy, balanced, and purpose-driven life. Before working with Tony, I had a hunger and a drive to make something meaningful out of my life, but I was utterly confused by what that first step needed to be. I also lacked mentors and relevant role models who could give me the proper advice on what action to take first. I remember having more ideas than I knew how to manage back then, and going to work each day was an exercise in patience. I felt like I could accomplish more in one day than most of my coworkers, and for some reason, I was not getting ahead. Day in and day out, I pushed and gave my all, but the world around me wasn't adding up to what I would call success. I was far from living on purpose. But when I started working with Tony and the team at Robbins Research International, things changed. All of a sudden, I had been introduced to the makings of a successful life. I had a peer group whose energy matched mine, and whose drive for more out of life inspired me to stay hungry. I also had access to knowledge and continuing education that put matters into focus. The office I walked into each day had a bookshelf that was eight shelves high, each adorned with either Tony's books or learning tools designed for personal power and professional mastery. I devoured every last one of them. From learning how to manage my time to creating influence in my life, each of these products gave me what I needed to transform all that wild energy into results I could celebrate each day. Back then, if you jumped in my car, you would have immediately heard Tony Robbins playing over any radio station. I was addicted to the learning, and my life was a reflection of how a commitment to #goDo and take action on a daily basis will, no doubt, result in positive change. Ever since making the decision to work on the Tony Robbins team, my life has changed. I learned the valuable skill of goal-setting back then. I learned firsthand from Tony how keeping a journal and making it a daily practice to write things down made things happen. This is I where I learned how to #goDo, and even on my worst days, I feel fortunate that I was given access to so many tools back then that continue to shape me to this day. Thank you, Tony!

You never know where life will take you, but you do have more control than you think. Adding a daily practice of writing down what you want or what you see happening each day is a great start to putting the wheels in motion. Take some time to do this next exercise. The process should take less than five minutes and, if done daily, it will start to produce miraculous results almost immediately. I know that sounds like a lot of hyperbole, but give it a shot. You have everything to gain.

Journaling Exercise

Take a few minutes to make a **prediction**. Write down what you would like to see happen today. You can write several sentences or, like a fortune cookie, leave yourself a short phrase to reinforce something positive in your day. As you sit down to write, pay close attention to all the things that are going well in your life. How can you make them even better? What strengths can you start with to accelerate the areas of your life you would like to improve most? Be mindful of the big dreams you have and write out a prediction around one or two things that can (and you believe will) happen today to support turning your dream or burning desire into a reality.

As you start to explore your future, your fortune, and writing down a daily prediction or horoscope, consider any of the following questions:

Are you waiting for a call back? Predict it is coming that day.

Are you hoping to travel somewhere you've always wanted to visit? Visualize it, predict it will happen, and then write it down. I promise your fortune cookie will eventually crack open, and you will soon be living the exact words written in your daily prediction.

It could also help to turn your attention toward an area you are currently struggling with. Perhaps you are finding it challenging to kick in a new health and nutrition plan. What about your career or your finances? I remember using this writing exercise one time when I was having a hard time financially. In that moment, I had difficulty focusing on anything other than my bills, as each day I woke up wondering if that check was going to come in the mail.

This is when this exercise became so valuable to me. I would sit down each day and write down that I was going to celebrate going to the mailbox and opening a letter that had the exact check waiting for me. I wrote about how much relief this would give me and what it would make possible. Many times, on the same day I wrote that I would celebrate receiving a check or a phone call with opportunity, that check or phone call would actually appear that day. Try this when you feel like you need it most. It works. Ask me how I know.

Taking the time to practice this does not come without effort. It is something you want to schedule and anticipate doing each day. There is a power you take back when you simply believe you now have the control to create your future. On a day when it seems like all is failing, take out a pen and paper and create your destiny—write down exactly what you want and predict what will happen. Remember that what you are doing is the beginning of a practice, a new habit that will take time to work into your daily routine. Keep the practice each day and, like most things, it will get easier and start working.

10 STEPS TO CREATING A PREDICTABLY BRIGHT FUTURE

For those looking to shift their futures in a positive direction, have no fear, I created a simple list of the top 10 things you can do to #goDo a bright future. I created this list after modeling what some of the most successful people on the planet were doing. Working with Tony Robbins put me in close proximity to uber successful people. One thing I found about each of them is that they don't wait for life to happen to them. Each of them creates their destiny. They take life matters into their own hands with daily massive action and they #goDo. After years of listening to people like Keith Cunningham, Joseph McClendon III, and Loren Lahav, I couldn't help but adopt some pretty phenomenal habits. Along the way, I created a list to share with others, in hopes of inspiring the #goDo jolt you need to #doGood sooner than later.

As you read the list, pay special attention to the things you may already be doing. How can you leverage them even more? From the list of things you are not yet doing, which ones can you add to your daily routine? Which ones can you commit to adopting as part of your new identity and lifestyle?

To start, pick one. The moment you feel you have fully integrated this into your daily ritual, select another one that will give you the confidence and acceleration you need to #goDo even more. For my overachievers, find the one that gives you the most anxiety. Which one is it? Why does it cause that reaction in you? My suggestion, for those bold enough, is to start with the one that gives you the most discomfort, because it is likely the one that will provide you with most value. Ask me how I know.

1. Believe You Can

For those who want to #goDo and #doGood, you must first believe you can. If you lack the confidence and faith to achieve any goal you put in front of you, you can make a safe bet that you will likely fall short of achievement. One of the most important steps to getting whatever the hell you want is having the emotional belief that you can actually #goDo it. As mentioned in the previous chapter, I use my goal-setting practice as a means of strengthening my faith, which also strengthens my belief. Belief, too, is a practice.

2. Feel a Sense of Purpose

You must spend time attaching your life to a purpose. Publishing this book was driven by my burning desire to live a life of purpose. I found purpose writing this book, and I hope it has helped you, so far, get closer or reconnect to yours. Purpose is the feeling that you know what you are meant to do. You know what your gifts are and you feel compelled to share them with others to make their lives better. This, to me, is the purpose of life.

3. Chase Something Greater Than Yourself

For a great example of what it means to chase something greater than yourself, watch Matthew McConaughey's acceptance speech from the 2015 Oscars. It is one of my favorite videos to watch. In one of the most unforgettable parts of his speech he says, "There are three things that I need each day. One, I need something to look up to, another to look forward to, and another is someone to chase." I cannot express to you how important it is to wake up daily chasing some dream, no matter what it is. You can feel the intention and forward movement of these words and, from them, you get a sense that Matthew is still chasing dreams to this day. There seems to be no end to his purpose. Let's watch and see what he #goDoes next.

4. Find Your Tribe

Motivational speaker Jim Rohn has been famously quoted for saying, "You are the average of the five people you spend the most time with." This quote is a reflection of the law of averages that basically says the resulting outcome is the average of all the possible outcomes that are present. Take a look at the people you surround yourself with. How successful are they with their health? Are they healthy and happy? How is their financial fitness? What about their fulfillment around their careers or businesses? I could go on and on here, but do yourself a favor and write down exactly what you think you want your life to look and feel like. Then ask yourself: Do these people reflect that as well? If not, get out. If you fail to get out, do not be surprised when you do not have what you are looking for. It's that simple.

5. Educate Yourself

Educate yourself nonstop, because to successful people, the training never stops. I recently read that CEOs read approximately 60 books a year. If you do the math, that is at least five books a month. If you keep working the numbers, you will find that 60 books a year is equivalent to a book a week. Not everyone is a superfan of reading, so for those people, consider watching a short video each day about a new subject or skill set. You may also want to attend a workshop or seminar. I heard Tony Robbins say he fully immerses himself in learning something new twice a year, or every six months. Immersing yourself in some sort of learning is one of the best ways you can predict a brighter future.

6. See It

"Tennessein' is Tennebelievin'."

This is a little quote my good friend, Jan, used to say just for fun and, after hearing it for so long, I realized how much truth it had. You must take time to see what your future can look like. If you're not sure what success looks like to you, how will you know if it shows up or not? Spend time visualizing success. Imagine you have it. A great way to help you predict your future through visualizing is to take time meditating.

I know, I know, it is impossible for you to sit still. If that's your response, let me tell you you are misled and missing out. You can meditate at any time of the day. When I am on the subway or walking down the street in New York City, I spend time imagining what I want. I visualize where I am going next and what it will look and feel like once I am there. We all need to just stop making this whole visualize and meditate thing hard. Keep it simple and #goDo!

7. Remain Flexible

This is a great one for those of you looking for certainty in your life. The more flexible you are, the happier you are and the easier it will be to enjoy the future. Let go of those expectations and embrace the uncertainty of how life never takes a straight path to success. The detours along the way are sometimes there to remind you to reconnect to your vision. Remaining flexible doesn't mean giving up on what you see, it's merely a risk-management strategy to remind you that everything has a purpose. To get to yours, you must stay focused, amiable, and constantly learning. Nothing in life is guaranteed except our freedom to choose what we focus on and the meaning we attach to all things. Caroline Myss, a prominent spiritual and self-development expert, always recommends we "stop using the word deserve. Remove it from your vocabulary. Nobody deserves anything." Since watching her TED Talk, I have stopped using this word and am focused on removing it from my thoughts entirely. What can you appreciate more of today, while remaining flexible?

8. Be Persistent

I recently watched a movie about Ray Kroc, the man who modeled and expanded upon the McDonald's fast food restaurant idea from the original McDonald brothers. It was a great movie, but it is a sad story. The movie begins and ends with a record that must be some sort of motivational speaker telling Ray to remain persistent. The message reminds us that unused talent and genius are a cliché and those who celebrate victory may just be more persistent than others. The movie conveys just how persistent Ray was—it does an excellent job of showing you the many times Ray tried and failed, how many bright ideas he pursued, how many of them fell flat, and how many people laughed in his face along the way. In spite of all of this, Ray Kroc persisted and went on to celebrate enormous wealth and success.

9. Take Care of Your Health

There is no purpose without good health, and a life on purpose starts by being purposeful with your body, mind, and spirit. At any given time, you only have three resources available to you: Time, money, and energy. How much of these you have always depends on your health. I could write another book on the subject of health and the rituals I follow daily that ensure I am pursuing a healthy, balanced, and purpose-driven life. For the sake of time, I'll leave you with this advice: Start thinking about health as energy. The healthier you are, the more energy you will have to create, to enjoy, and to live life. Instead of looking at health through the lens of what your weight is on a scale, or how many days per week you hit the gym, tackle the concept of health with the outcome of doing all you can to create clean energy. Do whatever you can to increase and maximize your energy and I promise you will be #goDoing and living a life on purpose in no time.

10. Give Back to Others (#doGood)

One of the major reasons why I wrote this book was to give back to others. Writing this book was a way for me to contribute to the health and happiness of others. I was fortunate to have spent several years learning directly from Tony Robbins, immersed in an environment of people who were insatiable in their appetite for growth and success. The tools and resources I gained from that experience formed the foundation and reasons why I do what I do today. I realized I wanted to make my life about others and helping others achieve similar happiness. I know that when I look back at my life when I am older, I want to see not just what I made of my life, but what I made of the lives of others. That's how you #goDo and #doGood.

Journaling Exercise

Start predicting your future before it happens. Write down what you would like to see happen today. Pretend you are writing your daily horoscope full of great news, connections, opportunities, and celebrations you hope to experience by the end of the day. After you have completed the writing exercise, go back and read what you have written out loud. See if what you have written as the prediction for your day inspires you. Does it light you up? Does it make you want to #goDo, #doGood, and live a life on purpose? If not, I suggest making edits until it does. Those few edits will be well worth the journey. Ask me how I know.

Scan Me

#goDo CHARACTER

"Character is like a tree and reputation like its shadow. The shadow is what we think of it; the tree is the real thing."
—ABRAHAM LINCOLN

KNOW THYSELF

There's an Ancient Greek aphorism that stands as firm today as it has many moons ago: Know thyself. With so many distractions to avoid (and opportunities to seize), having a strong sense of self is *the* competitive advantage. People will unknowingly, and sometimes knowingly, do whatever they can to attempt to compromise your sense of self.

Ask me how I know.

The more you know yourself, the more you can confidently #goDo and live on purpose. At its essence, your *self* is your character and, not only does it define how you see yourself, it defines how others see you. Ultimately, your character determines what you will #goDo each day.

In the first chapter, you explored four key areas that help you live on purpose—identity, personality, goals, and decision-making. In addition to highlighting the importance of hitting these targets, you learned how creating goals and predicting your future combine to transform a talker into a #goDoer. The first three principles of a #goDoer—purpose, goals, and predictions—provide the fuel to get you from #goDo to #doGood. This next and fourth principle around character, gives you the acceleration you need to truly live a life on purpose.

Let's start with a brief history lesson.

Character has been referenced in a number of ways. It was originally used as a mark impressed upon a coin and, depending on the mark (or symbol), there would be a corresponding value associated with that mark.[14] Think about the coins you use as currency in your country as well as the value attached to each coin. What about the paper currency? What value does this carry and what significance do the markings have on others?

Aristotle wrote that character implied moral virtue or excellence. The virtues and vices that comprise one's moral character are usually defined as tendencies to behave in certain ways under particular circumstances. For instance, an honest person will have the tendency to tell the truth when asked. An optimistic person will usually state what is good or right about a situation over what is wrong. These behavior patterns are mostly understood as relatively consistent and somewhat fixed over long periods of time. It is also believed that their impact can last under a wide array of circumstances or under multiple conditions. For example, we are inclined to believe that someone who tells the truth to their friends but constantly lies to their parents and teachers can still possess the character trait of honesty. Inversely, we can make the similar assumption that one who often shows up late may also possess the ability to be consistently on time.

The Ancient Greeks later used the word *ethos* to refer to the beliefs or ideals that characterize a community, nation, or ideology. For many people, their ethos will determine what values they will work toward achieving as much as they will work hard to avoid.

Some psychologists argue that character is relatively fixed. They believe character represents a collection of firm motivation and traits that are demonstrated repeatedly when an individual

14   Internet Encyclopedia of Philosophy, "Moral Character."

interacts with others. In simple terms, our character is how we act around others on an ongoing basis, as well as how they consistently act in response to us. But is character really a fixed trait like some psychologists believe, or can you grow or change your character with time and thoughtful practice?

How do *you* define character? How do you define *your* character? While conducting some informal research on this topic, I learned that when I asked my peers these same questions, I received a myriad of responses. Some looked at me with suspicion, wondering what point I was driving at. When I asked the same questions of others, I was showered with a set of ideas and beliefs they had obviously formed years ago about themselves and what they valued. Some people, who I might have believed to be conservative, surprised me with progressive revelations about their spirituality and faith. Other people shocked me by sharing insecurities or limiting beliefs they held about themselves that I never would have known had I not asked them. Regardless, I found patterns in all their responses. Those who had a hard time responding seemed rather lost in the questions themselves. There was a confusion around the entire exercise, and I got the sense that they had never thought about the question of character before that moment. However, those who could clearly articulate the make-up of their character seemed to do so with confidence and clarity, almost as if they had thought about these questions before. The quality in their responses seemed to have energy and passion. I was enrolled in their passion and unshakable confidence in who they were.

I admit my character is something I have thought about my entire life. I would like to believe more people than not spend a good amount of time thinking about theirs as well. Like it or not, we all begin to explore our character at an early age—from birth we receive messages about our character from a number of sources including our parents, siblings, other family members, teachers, or others around us who feel more than free to verbalize what they think of us. We start to associate who we are and who we think we are with the words and responses we receive from others, whether they are empowering or disempowering descriptions.

My goal in this chapter is to give you tools to ensure the character you are connecting with the most is really you and who you want to be. Taking all the influences in our lives into consideration, it is easy to adopt a character you no longer want to be associated with. Like friends and jobs we outgrow due to the changes in who we become in life, you have the same ability to decide who you are going to be at any given time. You are in complete control, and the choice is all yours.

This chapter gives you the chance to let go of old characteristics by proactively selecting the character you now want or need to be. In some cases, you already are that character, but until now, you have not taken the time to identify with the descriptions or personality traits that make up that character. This chapter will provide you with a simple exercise to ensure you have designed a character for your life that is allowing you to #goDo, #doGood, and live a life on purpose. Curious? Let's continue on this journey to #goDo.

People who constantly strive to achieve something meaningful in life seek constant clarity and consistency with their character . Understanding character allows you to stay true each day to what makes you come alive. Successful people have an unshakable sense of character. They have a clear understanding of what success means to them and who they need to become each day to celebrate that success. Their actions reflect their character, and knowing thyself allows them to confidently welcome each new day. They look forward, decide where they want to be, and take actions each day to help them move closer to their purpose. Once you discover your true character, you become more selective in what you #goDo each day, who you surround yourself with, and how you spend your definitive energy.

MY STORY, MY INFLUENCES

Throughout my life, many people influenced my character. My father instilled a sense of honesty, integrity, and humility in me. This is a characteristic I have carried with me in both my personal and professional lives. My father's work ethic was always strong, and he was the first person to show me what it meant to #goDo. To this day, I'm surprised how hard my father works. At almost 70 years in age, you will still find my father awake at 5 a.m. each morning and effortlessly carrying out physical activities people half his age cannot attempt. And due to his strong faith, my father was also the quintessential #doGooder. He was my first model of what this meant, and I'm proud to have integrated his service-based view of the world into my own life.

My mother influenced me to be independent and persistent and to always make sure I was doing my best each day. She equipped me with the skill to self-assess and use self-regulation to guide me long before I knew its value. Like my father, my mother was a consummate #goDoer. To this day, my mother is building a strong legacy as a #doGooder. She currently travels to various countries around the world helping women in underprivileged areas start and grow businesses of their own. She shows them how to find their purpose through character, set goals for themselves, and #goDo. As they say, I guess the apple doesn't fall from the tree. In my case, these words still hold true.

Both of my parents played major roles in the development of my character, and luckily both impressed strong character traits onto me that have helped me #goDo, #doGood, and live a life on purpose. I am sure I have failed to say it enough, but I owe a debt of gratitude to both of my parents. Things at home were never perfect, but I know my parents did an excellent job of making sure I grew up with good character. And for that, I will always be grateful.

MY MOTHER

When I was a kid, I remember how my mother would ask questions that forced me to reflect on my behavior and self-assess my decisions. Both allowed me to determine whether or not my actions were in line with my goals, and ultimately reflected my character. This was my first memory of practicing what it means to accountable: I learned I was responsible for committing to the character I wanted to become, and that commitment determined what results I would celebrate in the future. I remember coming home from school after taking an important test one day. After preparing and studying all week (or sometimes cramming it all in the night before), my mom would check in with me the minute I walked through the door. Her first question would inevitably be how I did on the test. My face and body language always gave my answer away long before my words could. I'd look up at her with either excitement or discouragement. No matter what, my mother's response was the same. "Well, as long as you did your best," she would say. That stuck with me to this day because, deep down inside, I had built an identity that valued working hard so I could honestly tell myself I had truly done my best. It was important to me to study hard and push myself to do well because, based on my mom's belief, I knew I could do anything I put my mind do. Those words were so ingrained in me that they are imprinted into my DNA to this day. Persistence was a characteristic I had adopted at an early age from watching both of my parents overcome struggles in their own lives. It was a trait I adopted as a kid to help me also succeed, and it is the characteristic I still celebrate to this day. Thank you, Mom!

MY FATHER

Growing up, my father was (and still is) a Jehovah's Witness by religious faith. When we were kids, he used to have us regularly study the Bible. As a kid, I remember loathing every minute of it. While my friends were gleefully playing after school, there I was reading the Bible. I was either getting ready for church or preparing to attend another Bible study. While it seemed like the world around me was living life to the fullest, I was practicing faith. I had no idea back then how important this was going to be in my later life. More than 30 years later, I have finally found the value in faith. I almost believe this is by life's design, but I will save that for another book.

I was inherently competitive, regardless of the task at hand, so I made it a point to read as many biblical books as I could get my hands on. As a third grader, I could not grasp all the life lessons these literary works hoped to teach me, but because of them, I soon realized I was both equipped with a pretty strong moral compass and I could read better than most kids in my school. By the time I was in fourth grade, I was reading a book a day. I was an avid consumer of anything written by Judy Bloom, and I was outpacing my peers in a way I hadn't planned. By the way, Ramona Quimby can be some serious business to a nine-year-old.

By the fifth grade, I had started to read and write at a high-school level. No big deal, right? Well, this glorious gift came with the holy price tag of daily Bible studies and an early education primarily coming from the *Bible Book of Stories* and such childhood classics as Noah's Ark, How Lot's Wife Turned to Salt (that one really messed with my relationship to table salt), and a host of other greatest hits. I never realized how special my literary repertoire was until, maybe, middle school. All this high-level reading and writing inspired me to have the character to want to constantly grow and pursue knowledge as a habit. It is one of the main reasons why I do what I do to this day. Thanks, Dad!

WHAT'S IN YOUR WAY?

By now, I hope you have started to think of some of the early influences you have had on your character. Not all of us know who we are, though. Due to varying life circumstances, not all of us walk away with as many success stories as others and, in these cases, there is a need to understand a few ground rules. As you look inside yourself, what do you see? What characteristics do you find that may be getting in your way? Are there characteristics like persistence and integrity that you are celebrating? Let's take a look at a few disempowering ways character can take us off track.

According to Deepak Chopra, when most people look inside themselves, they can unfortunately find three things getting in their way: Confusion, distraction, and disorganization.

Confusion

Who hasn't found themselves confused at some point in their lives? These days, with so much access to information combined with an increase in opportunity, confusion seems inevitable. It used to be that we needed more information to make a decision. These days, we go through the reverse process of eliminating information to get to what matters most. Confusion is easy and leads to failing to set clear priorities because the path ahead is just too out of focus. How many times have you felt lost and confused in your life? Too many times to count? Join the club, because you're in good company. All of us at some point in our lives become confused; however, confusion can be overcome by implementing a daily practice of exploring what matters most to you as well as gaining a clear picture of who you are. As you begin to consider what you value most out of life and out of others, you will start to see confusion lifted from within and around your life. As confusion leaves, a new sense of clarity, vision, and purpose takes its place. This change can serve as the catalyst needed to #goDo and live a life on purpose.

Distraction

Like confusion, these days distraction comes in every form. We used to have more chances to escape confusion, but nowadays it's everywhere we look, from our cell phones to our computers, to the whirling life of social media around us. Reality and screen reality seem to never give us a break from distraction. But what are you doing to protect and free yourself? There's an app for that, right? I've read that the average employee can waste up to 60 hours each month on distractions in the workplace. Things like chatty co-workers, mobile phone notifications, and simply daydreaming can account for almost 800 hours wasted each year due to workplace distractions. Noise, social media, uncomfortable environments, and online shopping are stripping a third of the workforce from truly being productive. These same distractions are present in our personal lives, and penetrate our intellectual and emotional spheres of influence. The results are having an effect on our character, as signals and cues are hitting us at an all-time record pace.[15]

Disorganization

Disorganization can have as much of a negative consequence on your identity as distractions, and let me be clear, organization is a practice. Setting clear boundaries and rules for your time, energy, and space—and adhering to those on a consistent basis—are the stuff dreams are made of. I know, easier said than done. Disorganization as a rule can destroy. For now, just pay attention to where disorganization exists in your life. I will provide more solutions to disorganization in Chapter 6: #goDo Targets.

Do any of the above sound familiar to you? Are you struggling with the overwhelm of confusion, distraction, and disorganization? If so, any of these will get in your way of #goDoing. And I can promise that if your path to #goDo is already met with too many obstacles, you will have an even harder time #doingGood for others and celebrating a life on purpose.

What is the solution?

_____

15 Huth, "Employees."

As mentioned earlier in this chapter, I want you to introduce this fourth #goDo principle into your life, as well as integrate this practice of writing about your character into your daily goal setting and journaling routine. Each day, take time to think about your character. Ask yourself often: Is what I am #goDoing with my time in alignment with my character? Does this action I am about to take match the characteristics I use to describe myself? Are my thoughts and words congruent with what I value and believe? If not, know you have the power to make immediate changes. Below is an exercise you can complete to get you started on clearly defining who you are, what's inside, and what character you will allow to lead each day.

"Be more concerned with your character than your reputation."
—JOHN WOODEN

Journaling Exercise

Take a minute each day to define (or create) your character. Take some time to reflect upon what character means to you. If you don't take the time to truly understand who you are, you leave yourself open to be defined by others. Understanding who you are will attract the people, places, and things to aid you in #goDoing, #doGooding, and living on purpose. What mark do you want to impress upon others? What moral compass do you want to guide you to #goDo? What set of guiding principles, values, and beliefs do you want (or need) to subscribe to in order to #doGood for others?

Use a piece of paper or grab your journal to answer the below questions:

1. If you were to write a story about yourself as a character, what would it say? Write a few short paragraphs you would like

to use to represent your character. When you are done, go back and circle (or highlight) every word that is an absolute must for you (or others) to use when they describe you. What did you learn from this?

2. **I am** statements. Draft a few **I am** statements that will affirm who you are. Make sure the **I am** statements support your purpose and the goals you are currently working to achieve. For example, on a quest to physical fitness and health, you may want to explore affirmative statements such as: I am fit. I am strong. I am abundantly healthy. I am a health nut. I am a source of energy. I am sexy.

3. What do you value most? Create a list of your values. Write down as many characteristics as you can that are reflective of those you admire and would like to emulate. They could be the characteristics you already see inside of yourself. What is most important is taking the time to think, imagine, visualize, and write down your responses.

4. What beliefs do you hold onto that guide you in your decision-making and make up the character and identity you are living today? What beliefs do you have that you may not be upholding? Are there beliefs you see in others that you would like to adopt? For example, some of my beliefs around food, nutrition, and energy:

- I believe food is energy and the better food I eat, the more energy I will have.
- I believe to be in peak physical health I must move my body in meaningful ways every day.
- I believe that success comes from energy, so I must do whatever I can to create more energy in my life.
- I believe that buying good-quality, organic food is more important than buying processed and convenient food.
- I believe that pushing my body builds muscle, so I must push my body to grow in new ways each day.

RECAP

Up to this point, you have been introduced to the first four principles of how to #goDo and live a life on purpose. Each of these four principles reflects a step-by-step guide you can follow to turn any burning desire into a reality. By following this guide each day, you will start to see the vision you have for yourself begin to manifest into tangible results.

In Chapter 1, you were introduced to the core principle of purpose. Writing a purpose statement each day directs your mind, body, and spirit to find the resources it needs to fulfill that purpose.

In Chapter 2, you explored the principle of setting goals and how the simple act of writing down your goals can accelerate your #goDo success.

In Chapter 3, you learned that the best way to predict your future was to take matters into your hands each day by creating your destiny. In this third #goDo principle, you found a way to sit down each day and write a daily horoscope or a short and sweet fortune to guide you.

And finally, in this fourth chapter, the importance of character was illustrated as a hallmark to discovery and a catalyst to transform your desire to have, be, or do anything into a #goDo and #doGood lifestyle.

In these next chapters, we will explore the things that could get in your way, even if you have taken the time to read this book and follow the four principles described, so far. Anticipation is a key skill to acquire on your search to #goDo and #doGood, and I will show you a unique and extremely practical way you can invest each day into removing anything blocking your success so you can truly live a life on purpose.

Let's continue to #goDo!

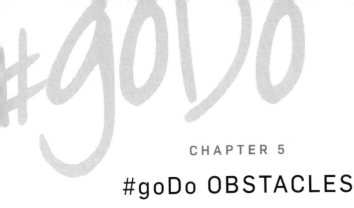

#goDo OBSTACLES

"To accomplish great things, we must not only act, but also dream, not only plan, but also believe."
—ANATOLE FRANCE

There is a reason why I took the time to introduce you to the concepts and exercises in character development in the previous chapter. It was important to have you pause and spend a moment getting acquainted or connected to who you are. For some of you, this may have been the first exercise in doing so. Have you thought about it much before that?

I've spent time throughout my life identifying with certain characteristics that were placed upon me throughout my formative years growing up in Texas. It was years later, well into my early thirties, that my mentor took the time to explain how important it was to proactively think about and write down, daily, the words you would use to describe your character. These words must reflect who you will and will not show up as on a daily basis. After practicing this principle for some time, I started to see shifts in my formation and perfection of self. These shifts went on the become the tipping point to other positive changes in my life, and so I added the habit of proactively creating and recommitting to my identity to my daily practice. In this chapter, though, I will introduce you to my fifth #goDo principle—identify your **obstacles** before they identify you.

I remember my mentor in New York City, a multi-millionaire who would get off phone calls to take calls from some of the world's most influential people, would tell me that your character is everything. Regardless of the money you have or the success you attain, it is your character that lives long past your life in this body. My mentor played a massive role in the management and growth of a number of successful individuals, so my assumption was that he firmly knew what he would and would not stand for. He had, let's just say, a strong sense of self.

I am glad I met him, and glad that after all these years, I can still share his message and the impression he left on me with others. He warned me that with character comes obstacles or threats to that character on a daily basis. I had never thought about that, in those terms, until we met. I am so grateful we did meet, because, to this day, I make it a habit of identifying potential disaster before it strikes. Again, as you read this chapter, think of these words as you craft an emergency plan that you need to put in place, as life will test you. Life will throw all sorts of obstacles in your way. Make sure you are #goDoing all you can to bounce back quickly. I am here to help.

KNOW THE ROAD AHEAD

As I mentioned in the previous chapter, character is something that follows you throughout the course of your entire life. It changes, it melds, and it transforms as you and your life transform. Along the way, though, things can get in the way. They always do.

What about potential threats to your purpose, goals, predictions, and character? What does it mean to have these threatened? It is not the same sort of threat you would encounter when someone off the street puts your physical health or life in danger, but the result could be just as disastrous. What if I asked you to drive through the most dangerous neighborhood in a city that statistically suffered from the highest rate of homicide? Imagine this was the deadliest street on the block and I required you to drive through it during a time of violence or crisis. Would you #goDo then?

What if I invited someone who was trying to eat healthier to a restaurant that only served burgers, fries, and milkshakes? How smart would that be? I could think of a thousand other ways to better support the health and well-being of another.

Knowing the road ahead enables you to protect yourself from falling into traps designed to cause confusion, distraction, or disorganization. We use tools all the time to help us prevent the unavoidable obstacles in life. We watch the news to see what the weather holds for us. We use GPS and satellite-driven location devices to help us avoid traffic jams or long commutes from work to home and back. But what are the systems we use to navigate our lives? What resources are available to us to ensure we get to where we need to go sooner, further, and faster while avoiding life's traffic jams? What anticipation tools are we implementing in our own lives to forecast the weather? Like seasons, we know that after fall, winter is upon us. So, how do we get through those unavoidable dark days and cold nights, appearing unshakable amid their harsh conditions?

This next section can be looked at as one of those tools, a sort of risk management plan for your life. Threats to our purpose, goals, predictions, and character exist in our lives on a daily basis. Here are a few ways to remain victorious in the face of their gale force winds.

"Locate the things that hijack your time and be firm in avoiding them. We only get one life!"
—Joyce Meyers

RISK MANAGEMENT PLAN

All human activities carry an element of risk. By preventing problems, the amount of resources, time, and cost spent on solving these problems can be reduced significantly. By adopting the mindset that you can avoid some problems by implementing a risk management strategy, you put yourself ahead of the game. Here is a simple process you can adopt to help you identify obstacles long before you need to.

Assess

Assess all the areas of your life you are working hard to grow and how they function toward your fulfillment and purpose. Look at your goals from Chapter 2 and consider what core areas of your life you intend to focus on growing. Make a list of these goals.

Focus

Creating a solid plan to avoid obstacles requires you to take a thorough analysis of your life the same way you would of your business or career responsibilities. What are the specific measurable results you are looking to achieve in each of the functional areas in step one? For example, are you currently looking to let go of unnecessary weight, or are you looking to gain weight through a thorough weight training program? What about your career? Are you looking to grow any part of your career? Think about the various components of this career and what needs to be operationalized or isolated for potential growth.

Plan

After you have identified the key areas (or goals that support your purpose), make a list of all the potential threats to your success in these areas. What obstacles are already standing in your way? What influences are currently sabotaging your success in these areas? What behaviors or decisions are preventing you from living on purpose?

MY STORY

Like many people, I have struggled with maintaining a weight I was comfortable with throughout my entire life. I was always somewhat overweight as a kid. I was nowhere near unhealthy or obese, but I was always just heavy enough to make my weight a source of insecurity for as long as I can remember. Throughout my life, though, I have always been active. No matter what weight was reflected on the scale, I knew remaining active was important. It is probably why, to this day, I am so excited to have a great relationship with fitness, working out, and consistent movement as guiding life principles. As a kid, though, I remember how unhealthy our diet was in my family. We were the typical American family who lived off processed and packaged foods and fast food restaurants. We lacked either reliable knowledge or intention around good food choices, or maybe we did not have the money to eat well. We had a lifestyle around fast food, which felt like a luxury to my child self. I remember it was a treat when we got to go to McDonald's. I wouldn't touch that stuff today, but in full disclosure: My biggest food obstacle to my healthy character is pizza! Pause. Let's take a moment of silence for pizza. Let's #goDo...

As you can imagine, growing up and reinforcing the behavior to reach to fast food for a source of nutrition haunted me throughout my life. This was a pattern that started in my family from as far back as I can remember, and I have had to work hard on crafting the right purpose, goals, predictions, and character to reverse the habitual wiring that has persisted over so many years.

Even during the early stages of writing this book, I found myself battling to overcome the cycle of weight loss and weight gain. It wasn't until I lived and breathed by these six #goDo principles and finally took them to the next level that I was able to overcome my persistent challenge of reaching my goal weight. I am happy to celebrate that, as of the completion of this book, I have finally reached a target weight and maintain a daily ritual that is helping me to continue to progress in the right direction toward reaching my ultimate health and fitness goal. The step-by-step guide in this book works, and I promise if you make it a part of your everyday practice, it will work for you.

It wasn't until I grew older that I became crystal clear about the role health played in my life. This was when I started to take health and fitness to an entirely new level. Health and fitness were no longer about vanity. Instead, I linked exercise to increased energy. This increase in energy transformed itself into mental clarity for me and an acceleration in my overall performance, both personally and professionally. In the end, the more energy I had, the more creative I knew I would be. And the more creative I was, the more I was living on purpose.

This journey started with daily exercise and a commitment to ride my bike for at least 45 minutes each day when I first moved to southern California in 2002. I remember how hard it would be to force myself to take that bike ride as soon as I got home from work, when all I really wanted to do was hang out with my best friend and roommate. I remember how hard it would be when the sun was shining and the weather was perfect (as it usually is in San Diego), and how I would have much rather preferred to go out with friends to entertain myself over riding my bike or going to the gym. Side note: I also remember how my roommate and I got on this nutrition kick. We were so hard core about it and forced ourselves to live off grilled chicken and frozen vegetables for who knows how long. But I have to admit, it worked and, at that time of my life, I was removing all sorts of obstacles that posed threats to my health and fitness goals. I guess carbs were a major obstacle back then as well. Little did I know that I was #goDoing even then!

Fast-forward to today. For those who know me, I have a sort of propensity to try all sorts of health and nutrition potions. I hesitate to call them fads or schemes because of the amount of time

I spend reading and researching about health. To me, these are not schemes as much as they are my attempts to hack my own health. During these past several years, I can proudly admit I am the healthiest I have ever been. I am not the lightest with regard to weight on a scale, but I am the healthiest. I order green juices to be delivered to my home on a weekly basis. I take supplements to aid in my absorption each day. I drink salt water with a potion high in polyphenols (ask me about this on a separate occasion), and I chug down at least three tablespoons of Udo's oil each day to support my cognitive function and overall levels of nutritional success.

I know, I know. It all sounds a little bit like a witch doctor, but the outcome I am ultimately trying to achieve is increased health and energy. Yes, I want to lose weight. In fact, at the time I am writing this chapter, I still have more than 15 pounds left to let go of, and I keep teetering between these 10 pounds I cannot yet seem to release. It's frustrating, yes, but my energy and clarity is at its all-time high. I sleep great at night and when I wake up I am typically quick to brighten up full of energy. I am ready to #goDo, #doGood, and live on purpose.

So, why do I tell you all this? Well, to get to the point where I am the healthiest I have ever been, I have needed to make some serious sacrifices. It has been a long road to get to where I am today. And there have been so many stops and obstacles to my success along this road that you cannot even imagine. These threats, or obstacles, are the everyday decisions that stand in our way of getting whatever the hell we want.

When I finally made that commitment to getting my health in check, I started with my number one motivator. At the time, that motivation was productivity. I was committed to being productive because so much of my life and character was wrapped up in my work. I defined myself and my accomplishments in life by how well my business and finances were doing at the time. So, in my search to #goDo, make more money, and feel more accomplished in my life, I decided to commit to increased energy.

I used increased success as my point of leverage on myself. For comparison's sake, some people use wanting to make their ex jealous as a means of leveraging themselves to get back into shape. Others find a way to get leverage over themselves by making it their goal to fit into the same pair of jeans they wore back in high school. But for me, my pain point or my biggest source of motivation was success. Yes, I am an overachiever and have been my entire life, but I used this as the reason or motivation to truly and finally get healthy. And, by healthy, I don't mean just losing weight. By healthy, I mean massively transforming the amount of energy I can get out of my mind, body, and spirit in a day. Anything that threatened my energy was considered an enemy.

For me to transform and get better results, I had to transform all the things that were standing in my way. I had to completely get rid of some things, while I had to simply replace others. There was a time in my life when I used to surround myself with people who, let's just say, had very loose standards for health and nutrition. These were all great people; however, they ate and drank whatever they wanted. When spending time with them, I would be constantly invited to drink too much alcohol and eat unhealthy food.

As described in the Preface of the book, I've not escaped a life of poor decisions. I've dabbled in recreational substance abuse, and there also a time in my life where drinking was a daily habit. But, when I finally decided I was going to make health and fitness my identity (my character), I had to eliminate everything that stood in the way of that. This meant no longer spending time with people who made it perfectly alright to drink like a fish on a Tuesday night—the same kind and volume of drinking that would have you wake up the next day so tired, foggy, and dehydrated that you might as well just stay in bed.

Now remember, my leverage point on myself was productivity. To be productive you have to be able to focus and have endless amounts of energy to get you to the point where you are producing at a high rate. Long story longer, I have since then either completely removed these people from my life, or I have dramatically reduced the amount of time I spend with them.

Not only did I have to remove people from my life in my quest to live on purpose, but I also had to eliminate some choices and behaviors that I, alone, was responsible for. In my quest to make health, fitness, and energy the focal points of my life, I had to stop engaging in behaviors or making decisions that would sabotage my goal. This manifested itself in a number of ways. For example, I had to stop going into restaurants that would throw me off track.

Mexican food is my jam. As a girl from Texas, we ate Mexican food all the time. In fact, my measure of a good Mexican restaurant is determined by two things: How good are their chips and salsa and how strong can they make a margarita? As you can imagine, because I have been so committed to health and fitness lately, I have had to almost entirely remove Mexican restaurants as dining options. Every so often I'll go out for Mexican food, but I have alternative food options in place for me to consider *before* I go out. For me to successfully go out to eat and maintain my commitment to health and fitness, I use a few tricks to keep me honest.

SAVING MONEY

I've been on a path toward financial freedom for a long time now. Being financially free requires similar discipline and consistency as getting physically fit and healthy do. There are people who sabotage your ability to save money because they love to go out to eat at every chance they get. Their behaviors or your own are getting in your way. Ask me how I know.

When I want to save money, I automatically eliminate going to certain places that will get me every time. Does Starbucks ring a bell? How many times do you go to get coffee and only buy a single coffee? How many of you buy a coffee, upgrade the size because you're in the mood, and then, due to the fact that you had one too many margaritas last night, you decide to order the orange cranberry scone? On top of that, because you did not want to feel guilty about the poor choice of the scone, you decided you would buy a bottle of cold-pressed green juice? In addition, you were there with your friend who was out with you the night before, and she bought the entire group of your friends a round of drinks last night. As a thank you to her, you decide to buy her a coffee. She also decides she wants some carbs to soak up all that alcohol and a green juice to lessen the blow, so she orders the same as you. Now, instead of the typical $3.50 you would have spent, your tab easily climbs to a stellar $25 or more. Do this one more time in a month and you are now spending an additional $600 a year in excess Starbucks purchases, not to mention the excess calories this adds to your bill of health. Let me provide you with another example. One year, I sat down and went through all my bank and credit card statements to see what I was spending each month on subscriptions. After more than two hours of scouring statements and canceling frivolous monthly memberships, I saved close to $300 a month in charges. I couldn't believe the excess that was piling up month after month. It's amazing how $10 here and $15 there will add up quickly. I must have spent the next two weeks bragging about my savings to anyone who would listen!

For someone who is working to lose weight and save money to reach financial freedom, these choices are complete sabotage. Does this sound familiar? Well, the good news is there is a way to stop doing things like this, while rewiring yourself with new habits. It is totally and utterly in your control, and you only have to change one thing and make one new decision to eliminate this sabotage. My friend, you just have to #goDo to #doGood. Do you #goGet it?

ANTICIPATION IS KEY

Remember when I asked you to drive down the most dangerous street in the city? What if I changed that story to tell you that I needed you to run an errand and the fastest way to get to that errand was through the most dangerous street in the city. Would you still go? What if I told you that I needed you to run an errand, but before I sent you on your way, I gave you the choice between getting there quicker by taking the street through the most dangerous street in the city, or you could get there safely by taking another route that would help you avoid driving through the most dangerous street in the city. Which path would you choose? My assumption is you would do whatever you could, in your power, to avoid the dangerous street even if it meant arriving a little later. If my assumptions are correct, you would likely pull out your smartphone and digitally map out a few other options. Like me, you would proactively look into alternative routes that would protect you against putting yourself in harm's way. The same process should be applied to your everyday success. Your everyday #goDo. Remember, obstacles are found everywhere.

The truth is that we always have a choice to make the right decisions. I read a quote once that shared the idea of the one thing humans have over all other species is that we have a higher ability to make good choices. This fact alone creates a superior distance between us and other species. When we use this superior ability for good, or to #doGood, we can get amazing results.

Journaling Exercise

"Defense is superior to opulence."
—Adam Smith

This next exercise will aid in your learning of the fifth principle to #goDo and live on purpose. Once you have practiced this one time, add it to your daily routine to make it a habit. Doing so will help you eliminate those obstacles that seem to stand in your way of success day after day, month after month, or even year after year. No more failing to #goDo our New Year's resolutions!

Step 1:

Take a minute to visualize an area or two of your life where you are struggling the most to #goDo, #doGood, and live on purpose. Really take the time to see in your imagination and feel in your body (or physiology) all the key areas of life that have become pain points for you. What are they? Get clear before you move on to the next step.

Step 2:

Write down what conditions are present when you think of this area that has been a challenge for you for so long. Who is getting in your way? What actions do you take that sabotage your success? How do you spend your time in ways that do not support you? When do you encounter these obstacles?

Step 3:

Create a short list of the new decisions you will make to remove these obstacles for good. Can you leave your credit cards at home, on purpose, to help you avoid spending money? Can you review a restaurant's menu in advance to help you pick healthy foods to eat before you arrive for dinner? What else can you do to know the road ahead and avoid the bad weather, traffic jams, or system failures in your life? Take the time to identify all the ways that you can overcome these obstacles.

SUMMARY

Up to this point, you have learned how to proactively assess anything that can get in your way of success. This chapter is dedicated to things that threaten you living your life's purpose and celebrating who you become as you journey to reach your goals. This chapter has also shared a daily writing practice that allows you to identify any obstacle before it strikes. In the next chapter, we discover how to create targets to hit to accelerate our success. This next chapter is the how to guide of setting the right intentions each day that save you time, money, and energy. Let's face it, these resources can at times be limited, so let me introduce you to the next phase of your ultimate success story.

Let's #goDo, my friends...

CHAPTER 6:

#goDo TARGETS

"To infinity and beyond!"
—BUZZ LIGHTYEAR

TO-DO OR NOT-TO-DO LIST

In the first five chapters so far, we have walked through a number of new ideas and concepts to help you #goDo, #doGood, and ultimately live a life on purpose. In this next chapter, I will take the time to introduce the concept of targets to you. This concept of targets is the path most people start with when pursuing any goal, outcome, or result—they confuse making a list (or staying busy) with hitting targets that make goals come to life. Think about it, when people want something to get done, one of the first things they do is make a list, a dreadful to-do list. I intentionally waited until later in this #goDo daily writing practice and process to tackle this subject because it's important to understand the other five principles outlined in this book first. But no matter how many times I teach the six principles to #goDo, there has always been one person left clinging to their dreaded to-do list. This person holds on for dear life to their "I'm someone who makes a list then makes it happen" identity. Does this sound familiar? My assumption is that I'm either describing you or someone you know to a T. In my opinion, to-do lists are the things that kill most dreams because, in life, there will never be nothing left to #goDo. Think about it, when was the last time you crawled into bed and said to yourself, "That's it! I've done it all. Nothing left to do here!" Never.

I mean, never ever. Well, there will be one time when you will have nothing left to do, but that typically means you will never have anything left to #goDo again. Do you catch my drift?

There is a difference between making a to-do list and writing things down to get them out of your head. A to-do list, as mentioned above, is an infinite list of action items or tasks in any given day, week, month, or year. To me, the lists can go on forever, which is the main reason why I avoid making them. If you are someone who lives and dies by a to-do list, might I suggest making them shorter? Perhaps try writing up to 10 items on your list, to start. Keep it simple, right?

Just the other day, I led a training with a leading organization in Brooklyn, New York, and one of the participants confessed to regularly making to-do lists that could span up to four pages. That's right, four pages. I don't know about you, but I am exhausted and overwhelmed just thinking about it. In defense of to-do lists though, the principle of writing things down is a beneficial tool to leverage. If this book serves as your entry point to goal setting or a daily writing or journaling practice, it is a great idea to start the process by simply writing things down.

Writing down your thoughts, putting action items down on paper and getting them out will show you right away how to simplify all the things you are thinking about. The brain has a funny way of showing us multiple ways of saying the same thing. The best way to say one thing is to write it down. After practicing the habit of writing things down for a while, you will start to see patterns. These patterns represent the many ways your brain has been saying the same thing all along. And after some time, you will begin to simplify this on your own. Writing things down first, is the first step.

In addition to awful to-do lists contributing to the many reasons why most people lose sight of their purpose, below are the most common side effects of to-do lists. They typically cause people to:

1. Never reach their goals
2. Burnout quickly
3. Lose faith or focus on their goals

In this chapter, I would like to introduce you to a new way of #goDoing things that will help you avoid never reaching your goals, burning out, or losing faith and focus. After completing this chapter, my goal is that you will walk away having a refreshed strategy for how to use targets as an organizing principle for achieving and reaching your goals time and time again. Targets are designed to simplify the tasks and organize the actions you take on a daily basis to celebrate results. But first, let us learn the science behind this important skill.

FOCUS, FOCUS, FOCUS

Genius emerges out of focus. Genius is made possible when you limit your focus to one or two things at any given time. Unfortunately, most people make it impossible to reveal their genius by trying to focus on too many things. Your brain can only take so much, so it is important to know your limits. Sure, you can train your brain to push beyond these limits, but let's begin with what makes sense. Angelika Dimoka, director of the Center for Neural Decision Making at Temple University, conducted a study that measured the brain activity of subjects while they dealt with complex problems. Using scientific equipment to measure their changes in blood flow, Angelika found that as people received an influx of information and data to the brain, the activity in the brain responsible for making decisions and controlling emotions increased as well. When there was too much information coming in, the same part of the brain was triggered and suddenly shut down. The study went on to show that the test subjects started to make more careless errors as this happened. Due to information overload, the part of their brains responsible for making smart and quick decisions was immediately disabled. Have you ever tried to walk and talk on the phone only to find that you passed the store you were headed to 15 minutes ago? I cannot tell you how many times I missed my subway stop because I was more into the music or podcast I was listening to than paying attention to what was happening around me. I can recall many occasions when I could read that the next subway stop was the one I needed to get off at, but because my brain was overloaded with information, I failed to get off the train. It would be two or three stops later that my brain was able to actually process the information that had been sent to it much earlier. This happens more times than we realize. And now, thanks to social media and an Internet-everywhere society, it happens more than we would all like to admit.

These moments where we reach the break are becoming more and more frequent in most of our lives. The underlying issue is that we try to #goDo too much and most of the activities we do throughout the day are the very things contributing to the overload. Think about all the information, decisions, and choices we make daily. Go back to this morning and recall all the choices you were given in line at the coffee shop or even last night at dinner. The more choices we have and the more information coming at us at any given time, the more exhausted, tired, and less effective we become as the day drags on. Our brains have limited resources and energy to expend to make each of these choices. In the time between getting up in the morning and going to bed in the evening, an average person makes thousands of decisions, and each choice we make comes at the cost of draining our mental reservoir. With so many demands surrounding us all the time, and more coming at us each day, it's tempting to try *to do* it all and at the same time.

Our brains are optimized for switching from task to task, but when we do, our brains must halt any processing of the current task at hand and load a new set of rules for the next task. This process happens quickly, but all the halting, unloading, loading, and restarting takes a toll on our mental strength and overall capacity. Imagine running and stopping all of a sudden, only to sprint again at a moment's notice. I'm getting exhausted just thinking about it. Well, our brains go through the same stop, go, sprint, rest, and repeat experience. If we want to train our brains to perform better and more efficiently each day, we need to support that by focusing on one target and one task at a time.

MEMORY

Researchers have often debated the maximum amount of things we can store in our conscious mind in what's called our working memory. A new study puts the limit at three or four. Cognitive psychologist George A. Miller of Princeton University's Department of Psychology wrote one of the most commonly cited papers in psychology titled, "The Magical Number Seven, Plus or Minus Two."[16] Frequently referred to as Miller's Law, the paper supported the concept that the number of things the average human can hold in their working memory is seven plus or minus two. Working memory is a more active version of our short-term memory, which refers to the temporary storage of information. Each of us is given only so much space, so it's important that we remain mindful of what we allow to go in, out, and remain in that storage. Working memory relates to the information we can pay attention to and manipulate at any given time. My interpretation of Miller's Law, and the reason why I chose to include it in this book, is that for us to be truly successful, we need to make a commitment to focus on less. Although our brains can handle a ton of information, for us to decipher some things from others and to drive them toward completion, it's best to keep them short, selective, and few.

....

16   Wikipedia, "Magical."

READY, FIRE, AIM

I hope that by now I have made a clear case against multitasking and overloading the brain with too many *to-dos*. I now want to provide you with a vital key to clear the roadblocks that get in most people's way of goal acceleration. At this point in the book, you may have decided what your purpose is or at least what makes it up. You have also taken the time to get committed to, hopefully, a set of three goals that inspire you and support you living on purpose. Now is where the rubber meets the road. I want to introduce you to a special tool called chunking and provide you with more context around targets. I often use both concepts when helping others find solutions to time and project management challenges.

CHUNKING

Chunking is a tool I learned directly from my time working with Tony Robbins. He uses it to simplify what we focus on and what we #goDo on any given day. I remember working on an event with Tony in Scotland. He asked us to meet him to discuss what the plans were for the week. We spent close to half an hour walking him through the daily agenda and he looked at us with a sort of confusion. He then walked up to the dry erase board and created four boxes around four words. He said, "There you go. That's what we are doing this week." In less than a minute, he took nearly an hour's worth of work and chunked it into four words. I'll never forget that experience and, ever since, I've implemented the concept of chunking into my process.

Chunking is also a great strategy that can be used to improve your short-term memory. It involves reducing long lists of information that make it hard to remember down into shorter, more manageable chunks. You can chunk just about anything such as processes, commitments, goals, information, numbers, letters, lists, etc.

If you were to make a list of all the action items you think you need to take to hit a daily target or goal, there is no doubt you will start to see patterns. In Chapter 2, I shared that there are eight categories of life the majority of people create goals around. If you borrowed that list and compared it against any past to-do list, you would notice that things always fall under common categories such as health and fitness, career or business, love and relationships, finances, etc. For additional practice with this, go back to a previous to-do list you've created and see for yourself. I bet you will start to see chunks in your lists right away. Use those chunks to make life easier for yourself and, just like what happened to us in Scotland, you'll bounce down hours into minutes. #goDo!

TARGETS

The idea of targets takes the concept of chunking one step further. A target is something you hope to hit. The target may very well fall under a particular chunk where you hope to put your focus. For example, I may list today's target as: Push my body to build muscle and create more energy. This would easily fall under the chunk of health and fitness. Once I have that established, I can now list two to three tasks or action items to take today that will ensure I hit that target. Targets help you systematize your day in a way that will allow you to put your full focus on the tasks that need it most. These same targets will help you get a sense of what each day should look like to fulfill on your goals and live on purpose. Once you know that your goals are aligned with your purpose, you can start the daily practice of identifying targets that require executing daily tasks. Both will focus your aim.

TASKS

Focus on doing a few tasks well, rather than drafting a laundry list of things that stand no chance of getting done. But wait, the more items you mark off your to-do list, the more productive you are, right? Busy is the goal, right? Wrong. From here on out, let's agree that busy is a new four-letter word. Replace busy with focused and you are in business! I keep my daily tasks to no fewer than 3 and no more than 10 items. Sometimes my tasks are as simple as eating foods that are clean and full of energy or drinking plenty of water. By keeping your tasks limited and full of impact, you are making it easier to see and feel progress throughout each day. No matter what, my list of tasks should support hitting my targets each day. And my daily targets are aligned with my goals and, above all, are congruent with living on purpose. It's simple, right? No sense in making it any harder than it needs to be. Let's keep #goDoing!

If you pack your schedule so full of things, know that only some of what you #goDo will get your full attention. Make sure you are keeping your limited resources in mind as you preserve energy to go toward the targets that matter most. A former coach of mine used to tell me that my mind was like an art museum. It only had so much room on the walls to hang pictures, so I needed to be careful and mindful about what I would allow in the gallery. He warned me to make sure to guard what pictures I hung, as those pictures would get most of my attention. I still use this analogy of curating the walls in the gallery of my mind with images, tasks, and targets that make up a museum I could be proud of. What does your gallery look like?

PUTTING IT ALL TOGETHER

Thankfully, by now you have taken time to explore the categories of your life where you want to #goDo and live on purpose. Now I want you to transfer what you learned in Chapter 2 into a daily target and action plan. This daily plan will allow you to apply the sixth and final #goDo principle into a daily program that will, at its essence, buy back your time. As with everything we have learned so far, this last step is a practice. Like a muscle, it must be used, pushed, and flexed to grow. To be a successful #goDoer, you will want to sit down each day to practice using this muscle. Be sure to schedule 10 to 15 minutes each day to dedicate to writing down your daily goals, chunks, targets, and action items. Make sure to keep the lists short and focused. Ask yourself: Is it important that I accomplish this task today? How will completing this task help me hit my target today? Will hitting this target help me accomplish one of my three goals sooner than later? Will these things help me live on purpose? If your answer to any of these questions is no, all you need to do is course correct. Delete a task. Replace a target with another target that makes more sense. Stop making life so hard on yourself, throw away those to-do lists, and #goDo. There is a world of #doGooders waiting for you to join them!

Journaling Exercise

Take out your journal or a piece of paper and write down three major targets that are important for you to hit today to help you reach your goals. Once you have identified these targets, fill in each target with a list of at least 3 and no more than 10 action items or tasks that will support hitting the target for the day. Doing this practice daily will start to change the way you think about taking immediate action. Soon, you will condition your brain and behavior to be more intentional with how you spend your time, as well as what you spend your time #goDoing. Remember, this is a practice.

#goDo!

#goDo TARGETS

TARGET 1: _____

Task 1 _____

Task 2 _____

Task 3 _____

TARGET 2: _____

Task 1 _____

Task 2 _____

Task 3 _____

TARGET 3: _____

Task 1 _____

Task 2 _____

Task 3 _____

~~~~~~

BONUS

5 RESOURCES MORE
IMPORTANT THAN MONEY

I was talking with a friend of mine who was feeling stuck in her life. She was searching endlessly for the "next big thing," her next move toward brilliance and financial freedom! Sounds like a dream come true to me.

But what was she going to #goDo? Was she supposed to write a book like me? Was she supposed to go back to school? Maybe she should take this course or immerse herself in that class or seminar? Who the hell knows? I surely do not.

But, who hasn't felt stuck at some point in their life?

Many times, along the path to where I am today, I found myself worried about money and what was next. How was I going to afford to pay for things I needed (or wanted)? Where was I going to get the work, job, contracts, clients, and cash? How was I going to make it? What if I failed? What if I was a failure?

Unfortunately, many people focus on money as the ultimate resource. Money is hoisted onto this imaginary pedestal of importance. By doing this, people forget about the other currencies available to them that are just as important to accomplish any goal. When you take inventory of exactly what's needed to get to the next step, you soon realize that money isn't that important. It's just not the only tool in the toolbox.

Yes, I said it. The almighty dollar, as intoxicating as it may be, is nothing compared to the other resources you already have at your fingertips. Unfortunately, my friend, you're just not paying close enough attention. Let's face it. You may not be paying attention at all.

Allow me to introduce you to money's five currency relatives and the hidden rules around them:

Time

Are you unemployed? Did your employer just cut your hours in half? Did your business just file for bankruptcy? What about the company you work for? Did they just downsize? (That's "right-size" for those of you politically correct CEOs reading this.)

I won't make light of how horrible it is to go through any of the above listed experiences; however, they all have one silver lining in common: They all free up your time to allow you to focus on something entirely new. Let me say this a different way—when you lose a job or business, you instantly find time to pursue something new with even more passion, purpose, and possibility. That's amazing.

If you ask me, there is no greater resource or currency than time. Have you ever met someone who makes a lot of money who *didn't* want more time? I haven't. In fact, some of the most financially successful people alive wish they had more time.

Networks

When I was in college, I was selected to perform in the Disney Collegiate All-Star Band. Part of this selection came with the privilege to work with some of the music industry's most influential people. I remember walking away that summer with two quotes I overheard that have stuck with me ever since: *You are the net worth of your network. It's not who you know but what you do with who you know.* These are the best phrases to pulverize your lust for money.

One of the best investments you can make with your time, with limited financial resources both coming in and out, is to put it into meeting new people or reaching out to those you already know. If I asked you to think of three people right now who you knew well, who could help you in some way (other than giving you money), could you do it? My guess is yes, and further, I bet each of these individuals would give you much more than you can imagine just because you thought enough of them to ask for help.

Other than time, people are an amazing untapped currency. There are endless opportunities in what and who other people know. The network established through activation and connection to these people is infinite, and so are the possibilities for new financial gain.

Tips:

1. Join a networking group that will introduce you to new people and expand your network.
2. Make a list of 10 people you know and trust, then reach out to them by phone or email to connect or collaborate on something new. Sometimes, all you need to do is start a new conversation.
3. Allow yourself to be vulnerable—everyone can understand the feeling of being lost or in need of help. Allow yourself to be seen as such.
4. Research people with "dream jobs" or who work in fields that sound interesting or exciting to you, then call or email them and offer to take them out to lunch or coffee to "pick their brains" for new learning.

Knowledge

Knowledge is power. But knowledge not implemented is pure entertainment.

Yes, I get it. This book is full of penny phrases, but words become galvanizing for a reason. It just make sense to put ideas and knowledge into action. One of your greatest opportunities to grow your financial capital is to invest in new knowledge. And the best time to invest in knowledge is when you have the time and space to do so.

What if you spent this newly found free time investing in learning a new skill, strategy, or behavior? All you need these days is a smartphone or computer to get instant access to all the free learning your little heart and brain desire. Give it a try—think of one new topic or idea you'd like to learn more about, then Google it. What you'll find is more information and a relevant learning opportunity you have time to consume. Now, that's what my friends and I call a quality problem.

Tips:

1. Take a free online course.
2. Read a new book around a skill, strategy, or behavior that will help you grow as a person or professional.
3. Attend a free event that will teach you something new.
4. Pay attention to everything around you—there are no coincidences in life. People, places, and things that find you do so for a reason.

So, what are you waiting for? Google it then #goDo it. And watch what happens.

Experience

My assumption is that if you are reading this, you live a life that has granted you experience in one thing or another. Each of us has a wealth of acquired knowledge and experience. I bet you could fill pages and pages writing about celebrations and lessons that your last job, business, or opportunity gave you that others do not possess. This knowledge and experience could be shared, and it should.

Let's future pace this idea further—even if you didn't work for the next 30 days, I bet you could find a number of experiences to get into that would grant you a fuller library of learning, people, opportunities, etc. If you find yourself with time, consider volunteering with an organization that could use your time, skills, compassion, or interest. I guarantee you will not walk away feeling at a deficit. In fact, I bet you will leave full of gratitude, optimism, and with an entirely new sense of appreciation for the resources you do have. And gratitude is one of the greatest feelings you can experience.

Remember again, money isn't everything.

Money isn't important.

I say this all the time, but contribution is your number one success strategy. Focus on contribution and you are already facing in the right direction.

Journaling Exercise

1. Write down what your last business (or job) was and identify at least three new skills or gifts you gained from that job.

2. Think of one to three new experiences you would still like to make possible.

3. Imagine both the people and new learning you could take away from these experiences. Describe both.

4. Explore (and write down) all possible answers to this question: How could all these things help you with what might come next, even if you didn't know what "next" was? Use your imagination.

Energy

Energy is the source of all things. And, as Tony Robbins said, "Where focus goes, energy flows." Make sure you are focusing your energy in all the right places. Even if you are having a hard time finding time, recalling old or creating new experiences, reaching out to friends, colleagues, or acquaintances; you are always in charge of your energy and what you focus on. The best way to create energy is to get moving. Go for a walk, to the gym, to the beach, or even to the mountains. No matter where you live, change your environment and you will end up changing the energy around you. Doing both will force you to focus on new things, mainly something other than yourself.

I can make this promise to you: As soon as you pull yourself out of the abyss of self-loathing or fear, you can soon find a new sense of energy, possibility, and purpose. Once you get over this hump, you will notice that this energy can quickly convert into action—the action to call someone new, take a new course, attend a new seminar, experience a new feeling, or even give your time to a new cause.

FINAL THOUGHT

After you have put the six #goDo principles into action on an ongoing basis, momentum will build. You will experience shifts in the way you think and in the results you will start to experience. These principle create the foundation for anyone to become a #goDoer, but it doesn't stop there. The ultimate goal is to create a life of giving back, #doingGood. So let's explore what it means to #doGood, the path to truly living on purpose.

PART 2

#do6ood

#doGood MINDSET

"Don't believe everything you think.
Thoughts are just that—thoughts."
—ALLAN LOKOS

MIND YOUR MINDSET

Now that you have a clear understanding of the six #goDo principles that provide you with an effective strategy to live on purpose, I
can imagine you are hungry to get started. Before you start, I have
one more strategy to add to your toolbelt. The best part about this
strategy is how effective it is when applied to all areas of your life.

I am talking about mindset and the power of adding visualization to any goal you set out to achieve. Omitting this crucial
step from a #goDo lifestyle that lives on purpose would be similar
to purchasing a luxury car and forgetting to buy car insurance.
These work hand in hand, and together they can transform
your lifestyle.

When you buy any upmarket item, such as a luxury car,
you want the certainty that things will be fine in the event of an
unpredictable accident. Similarly in life, there will always be un-
foreseen bumps along the way, but when you gain the capacity
to see clearly in the face of fear, self-doubt, and uncertainty, you
gain a sense of confidence. Visualization is an exercise in faith
where you believe something has already happened because you
can see it as if it has already happened. Through the practices of
visualization, meditation, and what is called autosuggestion, you

are cultivating a mindset that supports your purpose, goals, and character. This powerful technique matches the conscious and the subconscious worlds to create new realities. Like I said, I view visualization as the insurance policy you need to turn what you can see in your mind's eye today into what you can hold in your bare hands tomorrow.

A lot of recent research supports the understanding of just how powerful the mind can be in its ability to affect the real world. Studies have provided us with the evidence to encourage the activation of the mind before the activation of the body if we truly want to #goDo and live on purpose; however, the two are not mutually exclusive. The power within our minds enables us to #goDo so many things that our bodies cannot accomplish on their own and, when combined to work together in tandem, the results can be infinite and astonishing. Our minds truly help us to live on purpose.

In the book *The Talent Code: Greatness Isn't Born. It's Grown. Here's How.* by Daniel Coyle, talent and genius have less to do with luck than they do with practice. The book reveals how three elements—deep practice, motivation, and coaching—work in partnership with your brain to grow a substance called myelin. Myelin is the microscopic neural webbing throughout the brain that adds vast amounts of speed and accuracy to your movements and thoughts. Scientific research discovered that myelin might just be the holy grail of achievement: The very thing that makes all forms of greatness possible, from Annie Leibovitz's photography to Serena Williams's sports performance. What I found fascinating about myelin is that it isn't fixed at birth. Quite the contrary, as research has found that you can grow myelin based on how you use practice and focus. And, just like anything that grows, what's grown can be cultivated and nourished. Where focus goes, energy flows, right?

Coyle goes on to write that deep practice can feel like a lot of work. He compares this sort of deep practice to making your way around a dark room. Entering a dark room starts with an uncomfortable process of getting your bearings. At first, we all bump into objects, feeling our way around the room until we finally start to stabilize. After a while, we can sort of predict what the room will feel like. Our minds and bodies memorize the sensations and actions until we reach the point where we can navigate that same dark room quickly and confidently. Deep practice models a similar process of adoption. What I also found interesting in Coyle's book was how our brains can repair and regenerate myelin. It strengthens and grows bigger, similar to muscle tissues. As it grows, so does our cognitive ability. This is great news for anyone looking for a unique cognitive advantage, and for those who may have lost any cognition.

I thought this book was intriguing because it single-handedly eliminated many of the fears we associate with growing old. The research conducted throughout *The Talent Code* shows us that we can grow the myelin in our brains at any age. Through practice comes strength. Just like anything in life, if you use it you can grow it, no matter what age you are.

The mind and the brain have endless uses that are fascinating. By using the power of our minds, we can positively (or negatively) affect our biological functioning. Not only can our minds influence the health and fitness of our bodies, but we can train our minds to positively affect our relationship with others, the way we learn, and the way our bodies heal or recover from pain. People all around the world also use the power of visualization to imagine themselves healed or healing from illness and disease. The strategy involved can be as easy as focusing on wellness instead of illness.

You can even use visualization to give you extra confidence. You can imagine yourself in a situation where you would usually be lacking but see yourself acting with confidence, conveying the body language of confidence. I use this strategy all the time to overcome fear, self-doubt, and uncertainty.

Whatever you apply visualization to, you have more of an ability to shape your brain circuits and the physiology and health of your body than most people think. The mind and our power to visualize should ultimately be the first resources we leverage to design a truly fulfilling life.

Research has also proven that the brain cannot tell the difference between what has been imagined or visualized and what the body has actually performed in real life. In a study conducted in 1995, researchers used a unique test to prove that the brain does not distinguish between what is real and what is imagined. In this study, a group of volunteers was asked to actually play a simple piano sequence for five consecutive days each. A second group of volunteers visualized playing the sequence, rather than physically doing it. The first group had their brains scanned each day in the region connected to the finger muscles. The second group also had their brains scanned, but what the scans revealed was that similar activity was triggered in both groups regardless of whether or not they physically played or simply visualized performing the sequence. This is just one of many research studies completed to show us how similarly the real and imagined worlds are in our minds and in our real lives.

This is why meditation has become an essential tool used by successful people. No matter where you look, what article you read, and who you speak with, it appears that successful #goDo-ers everywhere are using the power of meditation. I can promise you I use meditation as a primary means to #goDo, #doGood, and live on purpose.

There are a number of ways to meditate, and the opinions on how to do it best can be overwhelming. But, as we have explored in this chapter so far, the benefits of meditation go far beyond having a quieter mind. Meditation will serve as a catalyst to a #doGood.

In addition to getting quiet, meditation affords you an

opportunity to get clear and more connected to your purpose. I love the sound of that! Take the time to cancel out the noise around you—and based on the obstacles we discussed in Chapter 5 there will always be a lot of it. What you truly want and what your true gifts are start to reveal themselves as you get clear. Our purpose, goals, and character come to life when we take the time to get quiet, listen, and visualize. Are you compelled to get quiet yet?

MINDFULNESS

You can throw a rock and hit 10,000 resources about mindfulness these days. Everywhere you look, people are using this buzzword to infuse a new way of #goDoing things. Corporate America and even the education systems are looking at mindfulness as a way to make the experience of learning and leading even more effective, enjoyable, and experiential. Talk about entering the Shift Age!

Although mindfulness is the hot word of the day, the power behind it is more than a trend to get you to spend more time in yoga pants. For the record, I spend more than half of my time in active-wear, so I'm guilty of looking for any excuse to put on yoga pants!

Imagine what you could accomplish by using meditation and mindfulness as a resource to #goDo, #doGood, and live a life on purpose. Remember that if you can see it, truly visualize having or experiencing something, you can have it.

This practice of meditating before journaling, before sitting down and putting pen to paper, is a powerful technique. You don't have to spend an enormous amount of time sitting in awkward silence to reap the benefits of meditation. I am suggesting you take no more than five to 10 minutes to get your mind primed before it starts to direct the outside world. The power of visualization forces you to take the time to get clear about what you want. Visualization allows you to first see the vision of what success looks like to you, whether it be reaching an ideal fitness goal or purchasing a dream luxury car, or celebrating the victory of starting a nonprofit organization. The fact remains, most successful people will share with you that the practice of visualization is one they implement on a consistent basis. Why? Because it works. It works like a charm!

Have you ever closed your eyes to imagine a goal that is really important to you? What does it look like? What does it feel like? How would it impact your daily life? How does it make you feel? Who do you see celebrating the finish line of this goal with you? Who isn't there (for a reason)?

Take a minute and think about the questions above. Close your eyes and imagine.

Remember, goals you can visualize and see in your mind are goals you can experience with your hands.

MY STORY

When I was in sixth grade, the nearby high school band visited my elementary school to perform for us. Little did I know, this was their recruiting strategy, and boy did it work on me.

Instantly, I fell in love with the idea of performing in front of an audience (insert Leo joke here) and I ran home to ask my mother if I could start playing an instrument and join the band. Although I wanted to play the clarinet, my mother persuaded me to play the saxophone. She promised me playing the saxophone was cooler than the clarinet, which soon became my shared opinion of both. Clarinetists, you know what I'm talking about. Saxophonists, you do too.

It wasn't until high school, three to four years after I had first started playing saxophone, that I started to actually sound like a real saxophonist. This was also around the time when I started to compete in local and regional competitions. My love for playing music, combined with my competitive spirit, inspired me to start showcasing my talent at any competition I could enter. It was then that I hired a private lesson instructor, who turned me from a squawking bird into a real musician.

How did he do it? What was *my* tipping point?

Before each competition, my private instructor would dedicate one of my lessons to teaching me how to perform with my mind, using the power of visualization to accelerate my skill. I would sit in the chair next to him while he played a pre-recorded version of the piece I was scheduled to perform at the next competition. He would ask me to close my eyes and imagine I was the one performing in the recording we both listened to. It was magical.

We would do this two or three times in a row until he could tell I was integrating the music, performance, and vision into my own psychology and physiology. For even more confidence and assurance, he encouraged me to do the same thing as I was tucked into bed, ready to drift off to sleep—again, I would walk through the entire performance in my mind. From beginning to end, I would imagine myself walking into the competition room, performing a flawlessly executed version of my musical piece, and then walking up to the judges to receive my first-place prize! I can't begin to tell you how many times this worked and how many times I walked away with a first-place medal. This stuff worked—again, it worked like a charm!

For those of you more physically than musically inclined, let me give you another example.

I once had a personal trainer who would ask me to visualize doing a physically demanding exercise. Let's just say, I've never been an athlete, so lifting weights and doing coordinated gym exercises were never my idea of a good time. Regardless, I would imagine I had accomplished my physical goal with success before I had done it with my physical body. My trainer would then ask me to perform the exercise I had just visualized. A majority of the time not only was I able to accomplish this exercise with relative ease, I could even push beyond the point he had initially asked me to reach (and many times far beyond the limit I had previously thought possible). The practice of visualization enabled me to go much farther and faster than I thought possible. I could see it happening, so I could make it happen. I used this visualization technique the night before triathlons, half marathons, or other races. To this day, I have completed every single race with success!

This practice of visualization is still a technique I use any time I am faced with a rather challenging or overwhelming outcome. Whether I'm at the gym preparing to do a difficult exercise or preparing to deliver a keynote in front of a live audience, I make it a must to take the time to visualize what success looks like from all angles. This insurance policy is worth the investment. Ask me how I know.

Journaling Exercise

Take a minute to visualize a goal or new level of success in each of the following areas of your life. Do *not* write anything down. Instead, give yourself enough time to clearly see what success looks like in this category of your life. What would you be thinking, feeling, saying, or doing if you were successful in each of these areas? Take your time with this exercise and be willing to #goDo it often. What you see will change as you grow and continue to practice, but make sure you are activating the power of visualization to help you celebrate a life on purpose.

Health & Fitness
What does success look like with your health? Are you focused on physical fitness, health, and/or weight loss? Do you have a goal weight, body fat percentage, or specific goal in mind? Take a minute to visualize what successful health looks like to you.

Finance & Money

How much (more) money would make you happier? What do you need to feel financially fulfilled? Do you spend money or do you save or invest it? *Exactly* how much money do you need to feel successful this year? Take a minute to visualize what financial success looks like.

Business/Career/ Mission

What does your dream job or career (or mission) look like to you? What are you #goDoing daily in fulfillment of your career? Do you travel? Do you work with kids or serve those in underprivileged communities? Do you work early in the morning or late at night? Take a minute to visualize what your career success looks like.

Recreation & Free Time

How do you spend your free time? Who do you share it with? How much time do you want to dedicate to recreation and other activities? Take a minute to visualize what success looks like in this area.

Love & Relationships

What does your ultimate partner look like and how do they act? How do they treat you and how do they treat themselves? How do you show love to one another? Take a minute to visualize what relationship success and love look like.

Time

Where do you spend your time? Is it at home or is it abroad? What exactly does it look like? Take a minute to visualize what a successful day, week, month, or year looks like to you.

Family & Friends

Whom do you surround yourself with? How do you treat one another? How do you celebrate and share good news with one another? Take a minute to visualize what success looks like with friends, family and other important relationships.

Personal Growth

How do you see yourself growing? What strengths and securities do you now celebrate as who you are? What new skill sets do you have? What are you most proud of? Take a minute to visualize what your personal growth and development looks like for next year.

Take the time to see it all happening, trusting that the brain is #goDoing its part to support your reality.

AFFIRMATIONS

It is a scientifically proven fact that you will believe more things you tell yourself than what others tell you. Take a moment to let that sink in. What *you* tell yourself when that little voice in your head speaks to you has more to do with what you believe about yourself than what anyone, even those you trust most, tells you. This is why it is crucial to condition your mind and your thoughts to help you #goDo and #doGood. We must make it a daily practice to tell ourselves things that set us up for success rather than things that create a path to failure. Confidence comes from what we tell ourselves, not from what we look like, the job titles we carry, or the cars we drive. Confidence and success come from the thoughts and words we affirm or autosuggest to our subconscious mind. We have the power and we are in control.

MY STORY

As I was in the final stages of writing this book, in 2017, my life hit a snag. I was almost three years into co-founding a startup company. My business partner and I were having an extremely difficult time getting liftoff with the company and found ourselves drained personally, professionally, and financially from the journey of growing a new business. We were getting beat up. It seemed no matter what we did, we got knocked down and hurled in the opposite direction of what we viewed as success. It was the perfect storm—money was draining like a faucet from our bank accounts, we were investing a lucrative amount of time and energy, and we were failing to see success or a light at the end of the tunnel. You could say these were challenging times for us.

Well into our third year of trying to turn this idea into a minimum viable product, we just couldn't seem to get traction. We felt defeated and our egos deflated. Here we were, two confident and successful individuals who just had a tough time converting what we thought was a great business idea into a profitable business model. What was missing?

I will purposely leave out detailed excuses such as limited access to capital—financial, human, intellectual, and social—and purely focus on our mindset. To be fair, let me start with my mindset. I will admit that feeling defeated time and time again had a dramatic effect on my daily psychology. I had gone from a self-identified eternal optimist just three years prior to a negative person. I had lost total control of my mind and allowed fear, doubt, and uncertainty to invade the walls of this precious gallery. I let external and negative influences occupy the valuable wall space in my mind over the strength and positive reminders of who I was and what my character believed and valued.

Then it hit me. I knew that as the Chief Executive of this company, if I ever wanted us to celebrate success, I needed to get it together in my head first. I needed to take control of what thoughts I would allow myself to focus on. I knew that whatever thoughts I focused on, especially under such emotional stress, would become the reality and manifestation of my external world. That was a dangerous place to be, so I looked for help wherever I could. I found solutions in reading books, watching videos, and consuming any knowledge I could on the subject of mindset. What I found was compelling, and I knew I would be missing an enormous opportunity to #doGood and serve others if I didn't include something on the topic of affirmations in this book. In fact, if you want to almost guarantee living a life on purpose, apply the practice of affirmations to your daily practice. It is a game changer. Ask me how I know.

After researching the topic, I put knowledge to action. I started by thinking clearly about what I wanted. I mean, I got crystal clear. I then committed to saying what I wanted in my mind once and then twice a day. Once I started to say it in my mind consistently, I started to practice saying it out loud. I would go on walks and start stating exactly what I wanted out loud so I could hear the words with my own voice, visualizing the result at the same time. Soon, I could actually see life starting to reflect the exact things I was saying quietly in mind.

It all started to get real to me. As I repeated this process day after day, the world around me started to change. It's almost hard to describe, but the people and things I needed to grow the company started to appear. Left and right, I was being introduced to the exact resource we had needed all along. My clarity around this was at an all-time high. We were getting traction. We were making progress and that progress was absolutely perfect.

Above all, I could feel just how far my mindset had come. I no longer allowed the negative thoughts to occupy my mind. I no longer accepted the fear, self-doubt, and uncertainty as *my* thoughts. Instead, the moment I saw them appear in my mind, I dismissed them and quickly shifted my focus toward the exact goal I was chasing. This worked. The practice pulled me out of a pretty difficult time, and I can credit this practice to saving my business.

As I am typing this chapter, less than a year later, I am celebrating success I could only dream of two and three years prior. Even though the business is not quite yet where we dream it to be, it is well on its way. I have the practice of daily visualization and affirmations, along with the six #goDo principles, to humbly thank. Please take this practice seriously. Don't waste time like I did because, the sooner you start this practice, the sooner you will #goDo, #doGood, and start living on purpose.

THE FUEL BEHIND THE FIRE

Through the power of affirmations and what is referred to as auto-suggestion, what's possible in life becomes infinite.

Great visions are not that hard to come up with, but committing to them and carrying them out is where most people fail to turn burning desires into celebrated successes. As I just shared in my personal story, affirmations are a great way to accelerate your vision into something you can see, feel, hear, and know as real. They work, but what is an affirmation?

Affirmations are short and simple statements designed to create self-change in each person who uses them. In my chapter on character, I left you with a short introduction to affirmations or "I am" statements. These "I am" statements can serve as inspirations as well as simple reminders of your purpose, goals, and character. They are also a powerful tool to focus your attention throughout the day, which, in and of itself, has the potential to promote and create lasting change. Affirmations are not only used for manifesting specific goals, they're meant to encourage a life filled with gratitude and an overall positive psychology. This is a never-ending life practice because, no matter who you are, your mind has the constant need to be watched and managed like mine did over the course of starting a new company.

Affirmations are so powerful because they are used to reprogram the subconscious mind to encourage you to believe certain things about yourself and the world around you. They are also used to help you create the reality you want—often in terms of making or attracting abundance in the form of health, wealth, love, and more.

Our lives are a reflection of what we believe about ourselves at a deep and subconscious level. Walter E. Jacobson, M.D., believes that affirmations can have a significant impact on the results and events we experience in our lives. Dr. Jacobson knows there is a unique value in affirmations, because our subconscious mind plays such a major role in the actualization of our lives and the manifestation of our desires. What is your mind manifesting for you at this moment? Is it helping you #goDo? Is it influencing you to #doGood? Does it allow you to live on purpose?

At a basic level, when we feel good about ourselves and have a positive attitude, our lives tend to reflect more positive results, just like the story I shared about my life and my business. Proponents of the "law of attraction" often refer to this as a raising of our vibrations. As we think positively, these vibrations raise with positive thought and the physical world responds similarly, bringing and attracting positive results to our lives. Not only are we what we eat, we are what we think!

On the other hand, when we feel bad about ourselves and have a negative attitude, we tend to engage in self-defeating behaviors that may cause negative outcomes, like financial hardships, interpersonal drama, or chronic illness. We all have thoughts, both good and bad, but one of the most unique characteristics we have been given as human beings is our ability to choose what we think. We have the power and control to choose what thoughts we will hold onto and those we will let go of. You have the power to do the same. Just because a negative thought enters your mind does not mean you have to accept it or continue to focus on it. You have just as much power to accept a positive thought that passes through your mental highway, so you might as well use it to seize upon all your positive thoughts. Your life and the people around you will thank you.

A team of researchers at Carnegie Mellon conducted a study that suggests affirmations and the practice of autosuggestion buffer stress and improve problem-solving performance in under-performing and chronically stressed individuals. Another way of saying this is that by using the power of affirmation, you destress yourself and improve your ability to solve problems. For those of you who own your own business, have high-pressure careers, or lead overall stressful lives, here is a solution for you to create flow in your everyday life. Imagine how your entire life could change just by reversing the stress that is created in your life due to over-whelm. Need I say more? Might as well. Let's keep #goDoing so we can start to #doGood.

WHY ARE AFFIRMATIONS IMPORTANT?

While positive affirmations are used to bring about a number of changes on many levels, from making money, to losing weight, to public speaking, these positive statements to self, if repeated continuously and over time, are presumed to convince you that the statements you are telling yourself are true. As long as you are telling yourself positive and empowering statements, you can use this practice to increase your overall self-esteem. I will go as far as to tell you that you can literally change the world around you by making it a common practice to affirm better thoughts, ideas, and beliefs. My life is proof that this works, and I owe credit to this practice for helping me write this book. It is the reason why I finished it.

Some proponents of affirmations also claim that when practiced consistently and intentionally, affirmations reinforce a chemical pathway created in the brain that strengthens the connection between two neurons. As this connection gets stronger through reinforcement, the pathway is more likely to conduct the same message again and again. Simply put, practice makes perfect. Makes sense, doesn't it?

There is a set of published studies that is frequently cited to suggest that underperforming students who engage in brief self-affirmation activity at the beginning of a school term actually celebrate an increase in academic grade-point averages. This exciting new work has uncovered the positive effects that self-affirmations have on our actual problem-solving capabilities when we are under high stress. Take a minute to understand what that can mean for you.

The study results vividly showed that participants who were previously under high levels of chronic stress had their problem-solving skills impaired. Surprisingly, under this stress they solved about 50 percent fewer problems in the task than those not put under stress. What I found noteworthy was the effect self-affirmations had on participant results. Specifically, certain self-affirmations could successfully cancel out any effects of stress or impairment of problem-solving skills. In context, you can use self-affirmations the moment you gain awareness that you are now under stress. As soon as you feel the pressure, your next instinct can be to affirm something of a positive nature to yourself. I use this skill all the time. The moment I feel myself slip into a state of stress, I recite the following affirmations, "I am grateful," and "I am peaceful." The longer I affirm the statements, the calmer I get. The sooner I can calm myself down, the quicker I can get back to making better decisions. My confidence and decision-making skills appear sooner than later. This is how I go from #goDo to #doGood.

Anyone under high stress can foster better problem-solving skills simply by taking a moment beforehand to think about something that is important to them. This is an easy-to-use and portable strategy you can roll out before you enter that high-pressure performance situation, which most of us encounter on a weekly basis. For my New Yorkers out there, you get to meet it daily.

DO AFFIRMATIONS REALLY WORK?

Of course they work. I would not take this much time to focus on them as an essential tool to help you live on purpose unless I was convinced of their power. As soon as I combined the practice of affirmations with my six #goDo principles, success started to occur at an accelerated rate. By their nature, goals require awareness and constant focus to be actualized. When you use daily affirmations to support these goals, it's like putting a colored tint on your glasses. The color stays in front of you and everything you see is filtered through this colorful lens. Through the use of affirmations, you keep your goals right where they should be: in the front of your mind.

We have already discussed that one of the major roadblocks to success is focus, and the regular use of goal affirmations will help condition your mind to maintain its focus on the goals you want to achieve most. After all, setting goals is not the hard part. Remaining focused and believing in your goals will always be the hardest part.

Actualizing your goals requires planning, perseverance, visualization, and hard work. Affirmations help you master the focus and visualization part. If you want to achieve goals of significance, you will need to focus on the end result. This focus helps you get clear about your purpose, the success of your goals, and how to go about reaching them. This is taking your #goDo and life on purpose to an entirely new level.

WHAT ARE THE BENEFITS OF AFFIRMATIONS?

A wealth of benefits come from leveraging the power of affirmations to help you #goDo, #doGood, and live a life on purpose. Below are just a few of the benefits many have come to associate with the practice of autosuggestion or daily affirmations.

- You elevate your awareness around your daily thoughts and words, thus reducing the risk of allowing negative thoughts and beliefs to slip into your subconscious mind.
- You increase awareness around the synchronicities in your life, which motivates you to continue the practice.
- Daily affirmations help keep you surrounded by the people and things you want in your life and can help attract even more of what you are already celebrating.
- Helps you keep the small things in perspective. In a world where distractions are constantly hitting you at lightning speed, you can easily lose sight of the big things that appear small and small things you are making too big.

Journaling Exercise

Revisit the goals you are currently focused on and support each with an affirmation you can practice saying daily.

1. Take a sheet of paper and write down each goal you are focused on achieving.
2. After each goal, write three **I am** statements to support that goal.
3. After you have written these **I am** statements, say each of

the three affirmations out loud until you find the one that means the most to you. Pick the one you are able to attach the most meaning to.

4. Once you have identified the affirmation that carries the most emotion to you, start to associate that **I am** statement or affirmation to the goal and, as you go through the six #goDo principles, take time to say your affirmations.

I like to say my daily affirmations while I'm out on a run, in the shower, or engaged in another activity that gives me the extra time to impress my goals onto my nervous system and deep into my subconscious mind. There are so many resources available to you about the best affirmations, but start small, think big, and #goDo!

Scan Me

#doGood CONTRIBUTION

*"Our ability to live great lives has more to do with how much we
#doGood for others than how much we #goDo for ourselves."*
—TALONYA GEARY

This book could not be considered complete without taking the time to discuss and share what matters most in life: contribution to others and gratitude. As #goDoers, we become myopic in our quests to reach success, and oftentimes we fail to remember the purpose of the journey in the first place. As we grind out work, day after day, it is easy to forget there is joy to be experienced in serving the needs of others through contribution. It is also important to slow down and celebrate what we are grateful for along the way. Both contribution and gratitude have become more valuable to me than money or material objects. I have grown to believe more in the power of serving others than myself while on my path to #goDo and live on purpose.

When I started on this #goDo journey back in 2007, well over a decade ago, I was on an egocentric path toward disappointment. The work I was committed to pursuing began to feel like an obligation as I chased self-serving rewards like money and meaningless accolades. It took me close to five years and enduring the grief of my brother's death, to transform my egocentric world into an ethnocentric world. Why do we always have to lose everything to gain something? It was then when I experienced the shift from wanting to simply inspire people to #goDo—to take action—into feeling an immense responsibility to influence people to #goDo *and* #doGood. It was no longer enough to just take action. I now needed people to take action to help those who needed it most. The action started with them but ended with contribution toward the needs of others. Through the process of learning how to bring new meaning into my life, I acquired the compassion to influence others to #doGood with theirs.

In addition to the six #goDo principles you can practice daily to live on purpose, all of them outlined in the previous chapters, I want this book to successfully articulate the importance of passing on what you learn to others and working to create a life of contribution. The peak of success, when you can celebrate reaching a level of mastery, happens the moment you realize your cup runneth over. It starts when you have confidence that you have now learned so much that you can effortlessly pass on your learning and experiences with others in need. This is what it means to #doGood. When you make #doGood the mantra of your lifestyle, you commit to sharing what you've learned to help others avoid the same pain and mistakes you've endured, or to simply help them accelerate their success and live a life on purpose. A #doGood life puts focus on giving over receiving, and the #doGood master lives life from a place of contribution and gratitude.

To contribute unconditionally is to live a truly celebrated life. This is a life on purpose.

CONTRIBUTION

Contributing beyond oneself is essential to fulfillment, happiness, and living on purpose. There are so many ways you can contribute, starting with contribution toward the everyday needs of others. Contribution takes shape in a number of ways to give. You can give of your time by volunteering. You can also contribute money, skills, or knowledge to organizations or people in need. Parents contribute to the purpose-driven lives of their children when they provide both a safe and loving home and a good education for their kids. Many people work hard to raise the best children possible, investing everything to leave a legacy in them. I'm often reminded of my sister when I think of the quintessential #doGooder. My sister, who had her first child at 16, has lived a life fully dedicated to contribution through each of her three kids. Over the years, I have witnessed my sister lead a life of service to others, always the first person to selflessly come to the aid of our family, her friends, and colleagues. To this day, my sister serves as a model of what it looks like to #doGood on a daily basis. Her actions, and how she pursues each day with a desire to give, inspire me to follow in her footsteps. I see how it lights her up to see others happy and I'm encourage to follow suit. My sister is my #doGood model.

Stephen Covey wrote in *The 8th Habit: From Effectiveness to Greatness* that, "Deep within each one of us there is an inner longing to live a life of greatness and contribution; to really matter, to really make a difference." This, to me, is the meaning of life. This is what it means to live a healthy, balanced, purpose-driven life. This is what it means to #goDo and #doGood.

Lee Bolman and Terrence Deal, authors of *Leading with Soul: An Uncommon Journey of Spirit*, agree with this view: "Each of us has a special contribution to make if we can shoulder the personal and spiritual work needed to discover and take responsibility for our own gifts. When you know what fulfills you, you are able to give of your gifts in a way that also gives back to you." No doubt, #doingGood takes work. To get you to the place where you can focus on serving others requires the commitment to first find purpose—your purpose—and that can take a lifetime. Your true gifts and the possibility of living on purpose rest in your commitment #goDo and #doGood. It's that simple.

THE SCIENCE BEHIND #doGOOD

We just explored the idea that helping others is a key to achieving happiness. When you #doGood for others, there is a sense of fulfillment you receive because the recipients of your #doGood efforts aren't the only ones reaping the benefits. Science tells us that you also win when you #doGood. There are a lot of benefits of #doingGood that go beyond just that "feel-good" feeling that you are doing the right thing. Giving has a positive effect on your body and health, as well. Studies have shown that when people donate to a charitable cause, the mesolimbic system, the portion of the brain that controls our feelings of reward, gets triggered. When this happens, the brain releases "feel-good" chemicals that further influence you to #goDo even more good things for others. This phenomenon is commonly referred to as "helper's high" by psychologists. I had heard of a runner's high before, which I still do not believe exists, but a helper's high makes perfect sense to this #doGooder!

CHARITABLE GIVING

Giving to those less fortunate is the true hallmark of #doGood behavior, and this behavior has been praised throughout human history. The obvious reason for this is that making even a small amount of sacrifice through giving can make an enormous impact everywhere you look. Charitable giving and contribution mark the beginning of legacies, and the rewards that come with their efforts are not only associated with those who receive. Research has revealed that the people who give experience a number of physical, emotional, and spiritual benefits.[17]

Arthur Brooks, who is a public policy professor at Syracuse University, did an analysis in 2007 that showed how people who

17   Biswas-Diener, *Positive Psychology.*

engage in charitable giving are reported to be significantly healthier than those who refrain from contribution. There is something fundamental about the urge to give, and his research showed that people who self-identified as contributors were 42 percent more likely to say they were happy compared to those who identified as non-contributors. In addition, 25 percent were more likely to acclaim that they were in excellent health. His research supports the notion that those who self-identify as #doGooders actually affirm that they're happier and healthier.

In the book *Why Good Things Happen to Good People,* authors Stephen Post and Jill Neimark wrote about how contribution can make us happier by showing the evolutionary benefits of contribution. They showed that when contribution benefits a group, the resulting feelings correspond with pleasure and happiness, leaving less room to feel negative emotions. Evidence has also shown that helping others can contribute to better overall mental and physical health, such as controlled weight, lowered blood pressure, and relief from depression and chronic pain. When I'm struggling with something in life, I make it a practice to quickly shift my focus from me to others. At a time when I'm feeling defeated, I can turn things around by reaching out to someone with a short, loving text. I can change the way I feel about myself in an instant by looking for a way to help someone else. A donation of time, energy, or money is all it takes to turn a bad day into your best day. Give it a try and watch what happens.

Even though many of us are taught from an early age, and most of us grow to believe and accept that serving others is a best practice, I want to make the case for just how much we can benefit from living a life that focuses on #doingGood. There are six benefits that provide overwhelming evidence to compel us to #doGood sooner than later.

One: Self-Esteem

I would venture to guess that nine out of 10 people would admit to struggling with self-esteem on any given day. The good news is that if you struggle with low self-esteem, your answer may just be found in other people. Other people? Well, reports have shown that people who volunteer can have higher self-esteem and better overall well-being than those who do not engage in volunteering. Whatever your motive might be for volunteering, the act has reportedly increased the health, happiness, and in some cases, longevity of those who #goDo. Experts explain that as we increase and strengthen our social connections through contribution, our self-esteem also strengthens. Although the benefits of volunteering can depend on how often and consistently we contribute, the more we do volunteer, the more confidence we seem to cultivate.[18]

A study explained how the volunteers improved their self-worth, self-esteem, and confidence as they uncovered a newly inspired reason (their purpose) to get up each morning. The volunteers also gained confidence in dealing with others, and more than two thirds (70 percent) of the volunteers said their contributions gave them a sense of significance and belonging in their communities, which is a key measure of social well-being. Significance can sometimes bring a negative connotation with it but, simply put, the feeling we get when we know we are making a difference is incomparable. There is also a wealth of evidence underpinning the positive impacts of volunteering. Here are just a few examples of how contribution leads to better health and wellness:

- People who volunteer have better mental and physical health than those who do not volunteer.
- Those who volunteer have lower mortality rates, greater functional ability, and lower rates of depression later in life than those who don't volunteer.
- Volunteering has a positive effect on social psychological

18   Konrath et al., "Motives."

factors, such as one's sense of purpose and autonomy, and increases a person's sense of happiness.

- The health benefits of volunteering increase with age and the act of volunteering may help individuals maintain their independence as they grow older and face increased health challenges.

- There is a causal relationship between volunteering and well-being. Better health leads to continued volunteering, but volunteering also leads to improved physical and mental health.

- Several studies have found that when those with chronic or serious illness volunteer, they receive benefits beyond those that can be achieved through medical care.

Two: Stress Reduction

According to the Centers for Disease Control and Prevention (CDC) of the United States, more than 75 percent of all physician office visits are for stress-related ailments and complaints.[19] Unfortunately, chronic stress is linked to the six leading causes of death: heart disease, cancer, lung ailments, accidents, cirrhosis of the liver, and suicide. One of the best ways to protect yourself and those you love from any or all of these six leading causes is to live a life of service and #doGood for others. In 2013, a study was conducted that examined the positive relationship between volunteering (#doingGood) and patients with hypertension.[20] According to the results, researchers found that adults were 40 percent less likely to develop hypertension when they volunteered for as few as four hours each week. Additionally, a study in 2010 revealed that the more money people gave away, the lower their cortisol levels.[21] Inversely, the less money they gave away, the

19 Simmons and Simmons, *Measuring.*
20 Sneed and Cohen, "Volunteerism."
21 Ibid.

higher their cortisol levels. Cortisol is partially responsible for weight gain, too, so for those looking to shed a few extra pounds, perhaps now is the time to invest in #doingGood? Next time you're feeling insecure or have a few extra pounds to release, consider getting involved in your community as a donor or contributor. The results will give you the momentum you need to #goDo and #doGood even more.

Three: Living Longer

For those who want to live a healthy, balanced, and purpose-driven *longer* life, make the decision to #doGood for more people each day. Researchers from the University of Buffalo found a link between giving and a lower risk of early death.[22] Their research found that subjects who provided assistance to friends or family members (tangible efforts such as running errands, helping with child care, etc.) reported less stressful events and, consequently, had lowered their mortality rate. What I found most compelling was learning how helping others created a positive reduction in mortality rate due to how the acts of kindness buffered the association between stress and mortality. It seems so simple. Give more, live longer.

Four: Being Happier At Work

If you are miserable at work, might I suggest you start looking into a new career, profession, or mission to pursue? In the meantime, it may be easier to contribute your resources to increase your level of fulfillment. A number of organizations these days offer purpose-driven extracurricular activities through Employee Resource Groups (ERGs), and I cannot emphasize enough how making the simple shift to join an ERG—where available—might just change everything for you at work. If your organization does not currently have an ERG for you to join, perhaps this is your time to start

22   Poulin et al., "Giving."

one. Is there a cause that means a lot to you? If so, starting an ERG to activate the collective diversity of your team might be what you need to love your job again! Imagine what it will do to inspire a #doGood culture throughout both your team and organization.

According to a study from the University of Wisconsin-Madison, people at work who are more likely to #doGood are also more likely to be more committed to and focused on their work. These same people also tend to be less likely to leave their jobs. The researchers also found that those in their midthirties who made helping others (#doingGood) a priority also reported that they were even more fulfilled with their lives when surveyed 30 years later. Think about it, that's a 30-year insurance policy on happiness! This particular study made a significant conclusion by revealing that those who help others are happier at work than those who don't. So, as it stands, creating a #doGood culture at work is great for business!

Five: Better Mental Health

I believe it is a safe bet to say most people have bad days. I can imagine that at any given time, there are a significant number of individuals struggling with some sort of mental exhaustion or other decrease in mental strength and health. I know there are days when mine is put through the ringer. The National Alliance on Mental Illness reports that millions of Americans are affected by mental health every year, and about one in five people struggle with some sort of mental health issue. After an extensive review of 40 studies on the effect that volunteering has on overall health and fulfillment, it was concluded that volunteering is one of the best ways to increase mental health. Along with other compelling positive conclusions, the report showed that volunteering (#doingGood) was linked to a decrease in participant depression. One of my favorite things to remind myself when I am struggling with the inevitable challenges of life is to remain focused on others. One of the quickest ways to pull myself from an unresourceful place of fear to a resourceful place of joy is to find a way to help someone or add value to their life. You cannot be upset and grateful at the same time, right? I don't know about you, but that's compelling information. On those days when I am feeling less than awesome, when my self-esteem seems to be taking a beating, I'll push myself to get out there, #goDo, and #doGood for others. Again, it works like a charm![23]

Six: More Happiness

It may sound simple, but people who #doGood become happier people. My life is living proof of this simple rule. When I look at my life and recall some of the moments I am most proud of, my mind flashes to the moments where serving others was the focus. I remember the moments when I helped a family member or friend who was desperately in need. These are the magic moments that shape our lives, and inspire us to leave a legacy.

According to Sonja Lyubomirsky, PhD, professor of psychology at the University of California, Riverside, people who perform acts of service once a week claim to have led happier lives.[24] You see, just one #doGood deed can start to #goDo the trick. Scores of studies basically all state the same thing: Give to get happy. The more you #doGood, the happier your psychology will be. The happier your psychology remains, the better overall health you experience. Great health equals great happiness. What are we waiting for? It's time to #doGood!

#doGood FOR LIFE

I could fill a hundred more pages sharing one scientific study after another to show you the neurological research on the topic

---

23   Konrath et al., "Motives."
24   Ibid.

of #doingGood, but nothing compares to you experiencing the benefits of contribution in your life. The goal of this chapter was to simply introduce you to the idea that you don't have to wait until you have reached the pinnacle of success to starting helping others. By deciding to dedicate your time, talent, energy, or money to advance the purpose and happiness of others, you will start to accelerate your own happiness.

In 2012, after working with Tony Robbins for several years, I noticed a huge difference in my life. My life before meeting and working with Tony was good, but as I examined it five years later, everything had changed. At that time, I was in a relationship I loved. I was traveling the world getting to see places and meet people who I had never imagined meeting before. My life was amazing, and what I found was a new sense of gratitude and a need to pass on this great fortune. Soon after making this realization, I started to host similar events as Tony, experiential learning events that aimed to develop those who wanted to join me, both personally and professionally. This time in my life was abundantly rewarding to me. I found myself giving away my time and knowledge to anyone who would listen, and each day I felt the fulfillment growing inside me. I had turned the focus of my life from a #goDo life to a #doGood life, and the rewards were infinite.

To this day, I look back at the beginnings of my #doGood life with gratitude. Those experiences shaped me into who I am today and, had it not been for those experiences, I may not be writing this book for you to read and share with others. We all start somewhere and the key is to start. #goDo and #doGood. Your future self will thank you and, as always, ask me how I know.

CELEBRATION

I like to buy things. Let me rephrase that, I *love* to buy things. I am the type of person who sees something I want and buys it right away, with little restraint, but what I noticed was how unfulfilling it was to do that. Sure, it *is* great to have the ability and privilege to buy something you want when you want it, but is it fulfilling?

In 2014, just over a year after I had moved to New York, my life had reached a new level of success. I was making more money than I had ever made before in my professional career. It felt like I had money to burn. I lived in Manhattan, and if there is one thing you can be guaranteed, it is that New York City will eventually find a way to get money out of your hands. At the time, I also lived in one of New York City's most coveted neighborhoods, an area littered with unnecessarily pricey cafes, amazing restaurants, and fancy shopping boutiques. When I looked out of my living room window, I literally looked directly into a Michael Kors storefront. Michael and I became very close that year.

It became a regular practice for me to ditch work early on Fridays to go shopping. It was a sort of therapy for me—I would walk aimlessly up and down Bleecker Street, looking for anything I could trade money for happiness on. Some days it was a new pair of shoes, others it was a new watch or sunglasses. Some days, I spent money on expensive flowers or other completely unnecessary purchases to reward my hard work.

After several months of this, I paused and thought about the life I was living and the ways I was rewarding myself. Here I was, I knew I was doing well financially, but my rewards were all in one form—consumption through the purchase of material objects. When I took a minute to reflect much deeper, what I realized was these objects were not providing me with the happiness I was looking for. Instead, I realized what I was searching for was pure celebration. I did not need *things* to make me happy, I needed to celebrate what I had by sharing it with others. I needed to #doGood.

This reflection hit me hard.

I am all about a life of fulfillment and a life on purpose. I preach it to others nonstop. I chase the "life on purpose dragon" every day, and what I noticed in that moment of deep reflection was that buying things wasn't fulfilling me at all. It never did. In fact, it was draining me of my passion, purpose, worth, and all the things I needed to fulfill my reason for being here. Instead, I started to save money, invest it, or simply donated it to charity. I started to celebrate the fact that I lived a life that allowed me the gift to decide which of these made the most sense. As I have previously revealed, and has been supported by data in the previous chapters, the benefits of giving far outweigh the benefits of receiving. In the end, why does success even matter if it cannot be shared and celebrated with others? There is no point in that to me.

As the high of buying things wears off, take close inventory of all the things that are worth celebrating. What choices do you have that others do not? What freedom does your life grant you that others have never experienced? What can you be grateful for in this moment? What does celebration look like to you? Who do you celebrate your success and happiness with?

No matter how much you #goDo, it will never bring you close to the same happiness or fulfillment than living a life of contribution and celebration. This is what it means to #doGood. This is what I wish for you.

CHAPTER 9

#doGood GRATITUDE

"Wake up each day with gratitude. Be grateful for the chance you have to dedicate each day to a better version of you."
—TALONYA GEARY

GRATITUDE

Alas, you have almost made it to the end. As I too have arrived at the end of what will forever be my first published work as an author, I feel compelled to add one more chapter. I had originally planned on ending this book with the previous chapter. After four years, three months, and a few days, a lot has changed. I've changed. As I look back over these past four years, I realize the book I would have published years ago would have been an entirely different experience. I would have omitted the stories that gave you the deepest context of my life. That version would have read more like a manual than a memory. It would have included less of a look into my vulnerabilities and humanity. I definitely would have left out stories that gave you a look into the darkest depths of my existence, and you would have likely walked away thinking I had it all figured out. The truth is that I don't have it all figured out. I still have to work hard each day to live on purpose. Just like you, a number of things get in my way. I promise you, though, that I commit each day to gratitude and investing each day into a better version of me. I use gratitude as a means of expressing life in a spiritual way. A deep and frequent practice of gratitude allows me to create the quickest shift needed in some of the most trying of times. As I started writing this chapter, I thought I would keep it simple and just give you my final words on gratitude, because getting to this part of the book and knowing it's so close to getting published and making its way into your hands left me full of gratitude. I am grateful that it took me almost five years to complete this book. I'm grateful that I waited so I could share with you the most open, vulnerable, and real version of myself, to date. I'm grateful for you, grateful you chose to read my words, advice, thoughts, and suggestions. I'll always be grateful for that. And finally, I'm grateful it's almost done. Writing a book has, quite honestly, been one of the hardest things I've ever done. But we did it. It's done. But wait, there's more. It's called gratitude.

GRATITUDE: FOR THE STRONGEST

Amy Morin, a psychotherapist and author who wrote *13 Things Mentally Strong People Don't Do* provides a great look into gratitude and how it, like contribution and #doingGood, is ultimately good for your health. The benefits of practicing gratitude are infinite, but let me share a few things to get you excited more than ever to integrate the practice of gratitude.

Each of us has an equal opportunity to practice gratitude. Awareness that you can cultivate the habit of gratitude is the first and most important step. The next time you feel yourself wanting to complain about your circumstances, try to catch yourself before you do. The moment you feel like you are getting the short end of any stick, think in an instant about what you are grateful for in that moment. If you cannot find something to be grateful for in that moment, what *could* you be grateful for? There is always something we can find gratitude in. Simply take a few moments to focus on all you have. Imagine all the people who would trade places with you in an instant, given the opportunity. We have all perfected a skill in noticing what we *don't have*, but spend as much time in gratitude for what you do have and life changes in an instant. Developing an "attitude of gratitude" is one of the easiest paths to #goDo fulfillment and live on purpose. Although some people wait for Hallmark holidays to be thankful, anyone can practice gratitude around the clock.

In Amy Morin's book, she shares research that shows how gratitude can have seven benefits. Similar to the benefits we explored in the chapter on contribution, each of these seven benefits are worth a closer look:

1. Relationships

A 2014 study published in *Emotion Review*, found that showing appreciation and gratitude can open the door to more relationships and help you gain new friends. The study found that saying thank you to new acquaintances influences them to pursue an ongoing relationship with you.[25] Taking the time to acknowledge someone or help a stranger will inevitably lead to new opportunities, and those who took the time to go the extra mile were typically rewarded the most.

2. Physical Health

Need a proven way to overcome sickness and poor health? According to a 2012 study published in *Personality and Individual Differences*, people who practice gratitude celebrated improved health. The study showed that gratitude helped people experience fewer aches and pains and report an overall better feeling of health. At the same time, grateful people are also more likely to take care of their health. They tend to exercise on a consistent basis and are more likely to schedule regular check-ups with their doctors, which is likely to contribute to longer, healthier lives.[26]

....

25   Armenta et al., "Functions."

26   Zeigler-Hill and Shackelford, *The SAGE Handbook.*

3. Mental Wellness

In addition to better physical health, gratitude can help to improve your psychological health as well. A regular focus and practice on gratitude reduces a number of toxic emotions, ranging from envy and resentment to frustration and regret. A leading gratitude researcher by the name of Robert A. Emmons, PhD, conducted multiple studies that revealed a positive relationship between gratitude and well-being. His research confirms that gratitude is effective at increasing happiness and reducing depression.

4. Empathy

Gratitude can reduce anger and aggressive behavior while promoting empathy. According to a study by the University of Kentucky, grateful people tend to be more social even in circumstances when others have behaved poorly. Those who ranked higher on the gratitude scales were less likely to retaliate against others, even in moments of confrontation when negative feedback was given. These same subjects also experienced increased empathy and celebrated a decreased desire to seek revenge. Imagine what we could do today with an increase in gratitude.[27]

5. Self-Esteem

We've already explored how contribution can increase one's self-esteem, but there is research to prove how gratitude can also boost self-esteem. A 2014 study published in the *Journal of Applied Sport Psychology* found that it was possible to increase an athlete's self-esteem through gratitude.[28] Gratitude was also used as an essential component for optimal performance in athletes. Other studies have shown that gratitude can reduce our tendencies to compare ourselves to others. Grateful people have an easier time

27   Ziegler, "Gratitude."
28   Chen and Wu, "Gratitude."

celebrating other people's success, rather than feeling resentful toward people who have more money or better jobs than they do.

6. Overcoming Trauma

Like the power of contribution, gratitude has the power to increase mental strength. Research has shown that gratitude not only reduces stress, but it can play a major role in overcoming trauma, even lowering rates of Post-Traumatic Stress Disorder (PTSD). A study published in 2006 found that Vietnam War veterans could lower their rates of PTSD by practicing gratitude.[29] A 2003 study published in the *Journal of Personality and Social Psychology* also found that gratitude could be used to influence resilience following the unforgettable terrorist attacks on September 11, 2001.[30] Even during the worst times of our lives, we can foster resilience simply by taking the time to focus on all we have to be thankful for.

7. Better Sleep

Having trouble sleeping or battling with insomnia? Instead of counting sheep, perhaps consider counting your blessings. You may want to start keeping a gratitude journal to help you fall asleep and sleep deeper. In 2011 a study was published that showed that spending as few as 15 minutes each day writing about what you are grateful for in a journal helps one sleep better, deeper, and even longer.[31]

GRATITUDE JOURNALS

I make it no secret that I am a big-time journaling addict. I've spent more than a decade keeping a regular journaling practice. This entire book is dedicated to a journaling practice to inspire

29 Monson et al., "Cognitive Processing."
30 Fredrickson et al., "Positive Emotions."
31 Lyubomirsky et al., "Becoming Happier."

you to #goDo and live on purpose. Did you know you could keep a journal just to practice gratitude?

Dr. Emmons, who was mentioned earlier in this chapter, led an extensive study on the practice of maintaining a gratitude journal. In his experiments, he compared results between those who kept a gratitude journal against those who did not keep a journal. In an experimental comparison, those who kept gratitude journals experienced better overall health and well-being. Those who kept the journal were more optimistic and felt better about their lives as a whole. They also exercised regularly and reported fewer physical ailments. Those who did not keep a gratitude journal reported more challenges or neutral life events, in comparison.

With regard to goal setting and achievement, those who kept a gratitude journal were more likely to have celebrated progress toward achieving important goals over the course of a two-month period. Each subject who kept a journal experienced more success in academic, interpersonal, or other health-based goals, compared to subjects in the other experimental conditions. Imagine what you can #goDo by simply taking the time to write down what you are grateful for each day. I guess we make things harder than they need to be. Instead, try making a gratitude list.

For those of you who have kids, consider a daily gratitude intervention, which is a self-guided exercise with young adults. These exercises reported higher levels of the positive states, alertness, enthusiasm, determination, attentiveness, and greater energy. Those who didn't participate in a gratitude intervention lost focus, tended to dwell on their challenges, and got caught up in comparing themselves to others. Children who practice grateful thinking also have more positive attitudes toward school and their families.

Dr. Emmon's study also showed how daily gratitude could turn participants into #doGooders. His study showed that these participants were more likely to report having served the needs of others. And in a sample of adults with neuromuscular disease, a 21-day gratitude intervention resulted in higher energy, increased positive moods, a greater sense of connectedness to others, more optimism, and better sleep duration and quality relative to a control group.

Gratitude Journaling Exercise

The following list of questions is designed to help you start a gratitude journal of your own. Feel free to add more to this list, and use the above examples to help you determine how to best start the important practice of maintaining a daily gratitude journal. For those of you doing this for the first time, consider committing to 10 days, to start. Once you have completed the 10 Day Gratitude Challenge, see how much longer you can maintain the practice. Make sure to document the success and benefits you experience along the way.

1. When you started reading this book, what did success, happiness, #goDo, and #doGood mean to you?
2. What do success, happiness, #goDo, and #doGood mean to you now?
3. If you could #goDo one thing today that your future self would thank you for, what would it be?
4. What is the best #doGood thing you could do today that would benefit the most people tomorrow?
5. How do you want to celebrate?
6. What are you grateful for?
7. What could you be grateful for?
8. How could you practice gratitude in a new way today?

9. What things can you #goDo that nobody else can #goDo?
10. Why is gratitude important to you? Why now?

Let this book serve as your invitation to start a new beginning in your life. Begin by adopting a #goDo mindset and living a #doGood life on purpose.

Are you ready to accept this challenge?

FINAL WORD

Believing in the right thing is no longer good enough. You have to #goDo it. Each one of us carries a special gift that needs to be mined. That gift, when cultivated, has the power to change history for the better. Again, I imagine you are reading this book to uncover that gift. My gut instinct tells me that you know it's there because it keeps you awake at night. You would do anything to share it with the world, and I believe you will. I'm here to encourage, influence, and inspire you to #goDo just that. Writing this book was a gift that I have been mining for going on five years now. I'm grateful something gave me the energy, focus, and belief to finally #goDo it. The words you read in each chapter are the result of that, and the reminder that you too must #goDo.

I tell people all the time that the only thing that separates you from your idols is that they kept going. Those people are the #goDoers who, in the face of fear, self-doubt, and uncertainty, made a bigger commitment to live on purpose. They looked at each day through the lens of a possibility to create rather than an opportunity give up. These same people defined clear goals, knowing success was just as possible as failure. And, in the end, they defined themselves by a character that #goDid.

Here's a toast to you, to your #goDo, and your #doGood. I hope this is just the beginning of your life on purpose. And may

you never forget that you can #goDo anything.
Ask me how I know.

10 DAYS TO
#goDo and #doGood

"Be very careful, then, how you live—not as unwise but as wise,
making the most of every opportunity..."
—EPHESIANS 5:15

This last chapter was designed to help you jump-start a new daily journaling practice in the shortest amount of time. You can #goDo anything for 10 days, right? The goal of this *10 Days to #goDo and #doGood* quick start guide is to allow you to create momentum quickly, and to help you navigate your way toward a life on purpose. I challenge you to commit to just 10 days. Make sure you are documenting the process each day. After your 10 days are up, you can then decide whether or not you would like to continue for another 10 or more days. Commit to the process one day at a time and see what happens.

Use the daily checklist that I created to guide you through your 10 Days to #goDo and #doGood. The goal of this checklist is to serve as a daily reminder of ten simple things you can be focusing on to get you increased energy, clarity, momentum, and, most of all, #goDo and #doGood results. This is where your life transforms. The following almost guarantees you will gain clarity around your goals, walk away with an unshakable identity, and live a life on purpose. Are you ready for the 10 Days to #goDo and #doGood Challenge?

Alright. #goDo. Then #doGood.

1. No alcohol (or drugs)—this goes without saying, but keeping the system free of toxins will help you to get closer to your true "spirit."
2. Eat a 70% or more plant-based diet.
3. Meditate, do breathing exercises, or yoga (10 minutes).
4. Engage in meaningful movement or exercise (20 minutes).
5. Schedule a time to journal daily and keep your word to this commitment.
6. Drink water and stay hydrated throughout each day.
7. Read for 30 minutes. (If you are used to watching television daily, start to replace that with reading. On average, I read about two books a month, which translates into non-stop #goDo acceleration.)
8. Document at least three celebrations each day. To start, you can think of these during your daily meditation.
9. Write down at least three things that you are grateful for today.
10. Find a way to help one person each day. This can be someone you know who is in need or a complete stranger. The bottom line is to #doGood.

"Repetition is the mother of skill."
—Tony Robbins

REPETITION

One final note for you in your quest to accelerate your #goDo and live on purpose. Once you have a new habit of journaling daily, you can start journaling more than once a day. Try journaling each morning and then again after lunch or before you go to bed. Use this time to reconnect with your goals, your day, and your progress. As I've stated earlier, many religions require their believers to pray multiple times a day. This is to keep them focused on their faith, mission, values, and beliefs. Journaling is no different. Are you ready to become a believer?

One of the most rewarding parts of journaling daily is when you are able to look back at the day, before falling asleep, to discover how much you accomplished or how much closer you allowed yourself to get to reaching your goals. Make the time to check in more than once a day and watch your results accelerate. There are few things more rewarding, and free of charge, than this!

If someone were to ask me what one thing I would attribute my success to, without hesitation, I would say it's a daily practice of setting intentional goals—with balance, health, and purpose in mind—and writing them down on a consistent basis. Although it took some time and practice, as all good things do, getting into the habit of writing things down helped me make it all happen in my life and made it easier for me to live on purpose.

I'm still not done. I'm continuing to #goDo and #doGood each day. The moment a goal is achieved, I celebrate and set a new goal and the cycle continues. Remember who you become can be the most important gain. Keep your identity close by as you prepare for the obstacles ahead.

It can be that easy. Now, #goDo and #doGood. It's time for you to live on purpose.

BONUS

#goDo DAILY JOURNALING TEMPLATE

1. #goDo: PURPOSE

_____
_____
_____
_____
_____
_____
_____
_____
_____
_____

2. #goDo: GOALS

01:
_____
_____

02:
_____
_____

03:
_____
_____

3. #goDo: PREDICTIONS (What will happen today?)

_____

_____

_____

_____

4. #goDo: CHARACTER (Who am I?)

_____

_____

_____

_____

5. #goDo: OBSTACLES (What's in my way?)

_____

_____

_____

_____

6. #goDo: TARGETS

TARGET #1:

_____

_____

ACTION ITEMS (Action items must support this target)

_____

_____

_____

_____

TARGET #2:

_____

_____

ACTION ITEMS (Action items must support this target)

_____

_____

_____

_____

TARGET #3:

_____

_____

ACTION ITEMS (Action items must support this target)

_____

_____

_____

_____

BONUS

1. #doGood: CONTRIBUTION
(How can I contribute to others today?)

_____

_____

_____

_____

_____

2. #doGood: GRATITUDE
(What am I grateful for?)

_____

_____

_____

_____

_____

_____

_____

_____

3. #goDo: NOTES & BRILLIANT IDEAS

_____

_____

_____

_____

_____

_____

_____

_____

_____

_____

_____

_____

_____

NEXT STEPS

My mission is to inspire and grow a community of **One Million Leaders** who #goDo, #doGood, and live their lives on purpose.

I want you to join me.

Are you committed to living a healthy, balanced, and purpose-driven life? Are you ready to get there with a like-minded peer group that will serve as your partners and coaches along the way? Are you ready to #goDo a life with purpose for the rest of your life?

If you're the kind of person who takes action to get what you want out of life—in the face of fear, doubt, and uncertainty—then this might be the best next step for you.

Below are a few ways to #goGet you there. Don't wait. #goDo:

COMMUNITY

Text **GODO** to **345345** to join our community of #goDoers. You'll receive relevant insights, relatable tools, and free resources direct to your inbox for free.

MEMBERSHIP

Monthly membership includes access to a private Facebook group, exclusive member toolkits and training guides, digital learning experiences, weekly live chats, exclusive live event invitations, discounts with program sponsors, and more.

To become a member, visit www.TalonyaGeary.com/membership to secure your spot.

KEYNOTE SPEAKER

If you would like me to speak at an upcoming meeting, conference, or other special event, please email talonya@talonyageary.com to start the conversation.

CORPORATE TRAINING & DEVELOPMENT

I cofounded Spiire, LLC in 2015 with a vision to grow thought leaders in the corporate space. Our goal is to prepare global professionals, teams, and organizations for future shifts in social connectivity, technology, decision-making, and capabilities. Spiire is a talent development company that delivers experiential learning events, leadership trainings, coaching, and consulting services to organizations committed to authenticity, inclusion, and innovation. To find out how to move your organization forward with Spiire, please visit spiire.org or email info@spiire.org.

PHILANTHROPY

A percentage of all proceeds from the sales of this book are donated directly to the below nonprofit organizations whose missions are passionately aligned with my values and beliefs. These organizations embody what it means to #goDo, #doGood, and lead with purpose. If you would like to contribute to any of the below organizations, please visit their sites directly.

THE SPIIRE FOUNDATION

The Spiire Foundation was founded in 2016 with the vision to cultivate LGBTQ Thought Leadership. The organization works to fulfill this mission through providing education, coaching, and mentorship to those in the LGBT community who need it most.

Visit: www.spiire.org/spiire-foundation

THE TREVOR PROJECT

The mission of The Trevor Project is to end suicide among gay, lesbian, bisexual, transgender, queer, and questioning young people. The organization works to fulfill this mission through four strategies:

1. Provide crisis counseling to LGBTQ young people thinking of suicide.
2. Offer resources, supportive counseling and a sense of community to LGBTQ young people to reduce the risk that they become suicidal.
3. Educate young people and adults who interact with young people on LGBTQ-competent suicide prevention, risk detection, and response.

4. Advocate for laws and policies that will reduce suicide among LGBTQ young people.

Visit: www.thetrevorproject.org

AMERICAN CIVIL LIBERTIES UNION

The American Civil Liberties Union (ACLU) is a nonprofit organization whose stated mission is "to defend and preserve the individual rights and liberties guaranteed to every person in this country by the Constitution and laws of the United States."

Visit: www.aclu.org

MIDDLE COLLEGIATE CHURCH

Middle Collegiate Church is a celebrating, culturally diverse, inclusive, and growing community of faith where all people are welcomed just as they are as they come through the door. As a teaching congregation that celebrates the arts, their ministries include rich and meaningful worship; care and education that nurture the mind, body, and spirit; social action which embraces the global community; and participation in an interfaith dialogue for the purpose of justice and reconciliation.

Visit: www.middlechurch.org

BIBLIOGRAPHY

Arison, Shari. "7 Scientific Facts about the Benefit of Doing Good." Goodnet: Gateway of Doing Good. Accessed November 2017. https://www.goodnet.org/about

Armenta, Christina N., Megan M. Fritz, and Sonja, Lyubomirsky. "Functions of Positive Emotions: Gratitude as a Motivator of Self-Improvement and Positive Change." *Emotion Review* 9, no. 3 (2017): 183-190.

Biswas-Diener, Robert. *Positive Psychology as Social Change*. London: Springer, 2011.

Blake, James. "Self-Awareness Is the Key to Your Success." Addicted2success. Accessed November 2017. https://addicted2success.com/success-advice/self-awareness-is-the-key-to-your-success/

Carver, Melissa. "7 Benefits of a Daily Affirmation Plan." The Chopra Centre. Accessed November 2017. https://chopra.com/articles/7-benefits-of-a-daily-affirmation-plan

Chen, Lung Hung & Chia-Huei Wu. "Gratitude Enhances Change in Athletes' Self-Esteem: The Moderating Role of Trust in Coach." *Journal of Applied Sports Psychology* 26, no. 3 (2014): 349-362.

Contrada, Richard, and Andrew Baum, eds., *The Handbook of Stress Science: Biology, Psychology, and Health*. New York: Springer Publishing Company, 2010.

Cooper, Aaron, and Eric Keitel. *I Just Want My Kids to Be Happy! Why You Shouldn't Say It. Why You Shouldn't Think It. What You Should Embrace Instead.* Late August Press, 2008.

Covey, Stephen. *The 8ᵗʰ Habit: From Effectiveness to Greatness.* New York: Free Press, 2013.

Davis, Jeanie Lerche. "The Science of Good Deeds: The 'helper's high' could help you live a longer, healthier life." WebMD. Accessed November 2017. https://www.webmd.com/balance/features/science-good-deeds#1

Deloitte. "The Deloitte Millennial Survey 2017." Accessed February 2018. https://www2.deloitte.com/global/en/pages/about-deloitte/articles/millennialsurvey.html

Emmons, Robert A. "Gratitude and Well-Being. Summary of Findings." Emmons Lab. Accessed May 2018. https://emmons.faculty.ucdavis.edu/gratitude-and-well-being/

Emmons, Robert A. "In Praise of Gratitude" Harvard Health Publishing. Accessed May 2018. https://www.health.harvard.edu/newsletter_article/in-praise-of-gratitude

Fei, Li, Jieyu Chen, Lin Yu, Yuan Jing, Pingping Jiang, Xiuqiong Fu, Shengwei Wu, Xiaomin Sun, Ren Luo, Hiuyee Kwan, Xiaoshan Zhao, and Yanyan Liu. "The Role of Stress Management in the Relationship between Purpose in Life and Self-Rated Health in Teachers: A Mediation Analysis." *International Journal of Environmental Research and Public Health* 13, no. 7 (2016). Accessed February 2018. http://www.mdpi.com/1660-4601/13/7/719

Fredrickson, Barbara L., Michele M. Tugade, Christian E Waugh, and Gregory R. Larkin. "What good are positive emotions in crisis? A prospective study of resilience and emotions following the terrorist attacks on the United States on September 11th, 2001." *Journal of Personality and Social Psychology* 84, no. 2 (2003): 365-376.

Froh, Jeffrey J., William J. Sefick, Robert A. Emmons. "Counting Blessings in Early Adolescents: An Experimental Study of Gratitude and Subjective Well-being." *Journal of School Psychology* 46, no. 2 (2008). Accessed May 2018. https://www.sciencedirect.com/science/article/pii/S0022440507000386

Gangadharan, Magesh. "The Ability to Foresee Problems and Preventing Them Much Before They Occur." LinkedIn. Accessed November 2017. https://www.linkedin.com/pulse/20140605145415-8716917-the-ability-to-foresee-problems-and-preventing-them-much-before-they-occur/

Gibson, Jeffarah. "A Life Lived in Service of Others." Tribune242. Accessed January 2018. http://www.tribune242.com/news/2016/aug/09/life-lived-service-others/?lifestyle

Hill, David J. "For older women, every movement counts, new study finds." University of Buffalo News Center. Accessed November 2017. http://www.buffalo.edu/news/releases/2017/11/014.html

Hill, Napoleon. *Think and Grow Rich*. The Ralston Society, 1937.

Hill, Patrick L. "Purpose in Life in Emerging Adulthood: Development and Validation of a New Brief Measure." *The Journal of Positive Psychology* 11, 3 (2016). https://www.tandfonline.com/doi/full/10.1080/17439760.2015.1048817

Houle, David. *Entering the Shift Age: The End of the Information Age and the New Era of Transformation.* Naperville, Illinois: Sourcebooks, 2012.

Hurst, Katherine. "Techniques to Stop Negative Thoughts." The Law of Attraction.Com Accessed November 2017. http://www. thelawofattraction.com/5-techniques-stop-negative-thinking/

Huth, Susanna. "Employees waste 759 hours each year due to workplace distractions." The Telegraph. Accessed on February 2018. https://www.telegraph.co.uk/finance/jobs/11691728/Employees-waste-759-hours-each-year-due-to-workplace-distractions.html

Internet Encyclopedia of Philosophy. "Moral Character." Accessed July 2015. https://www.iep.utm.edu/moral-ch/

Ironson, Gail, and Lynda H. Powell. "An Exploration of the Health Benefits of Factors That Help Us to Thrive." *International Journal of Behavioral Medicine* 12, no. 2 (2014).

Jaslow, Ryan. "Optimism protects against heart attack and stroke." CBS News. Accessed November 2017. https://www.cbsnews.com/news optimism-protects-against-heart-attack-and-stroke-study-shows/

Kashdan, Todd B. and Joseph Ciarrochi, eds., *Mindfulness, Acceptance, and Positive Psychology: The Seven Foundations of Well-Being.* Oakland, CA: Context Press, 2013.

Kashdan, Todd B. and Patrick E. McKnight. "Origins of Purpose in Life: Refining Our Understanding of a Life Well Lived." George Mason University, 2009. https://hrcak.srce.hr/file/74339

Konrath, Sara, Andrea Fuhrel-Forbis, Alina Lou, and Stephanie Brown. "Motives for volunteering are associated with mortality risk in older adults." *Health Psychology* 31, no. 1 (2012): 87-96.

LCS Approach. "Why Find Your Why?" Accessed January 2018. https://lcschristosapproach.com/leadership-why-find-your-why/

Lively, Kathryn J. "Affirmations: The Why, What, How, and What If?" Psychology Today. Accessed November 2017. https://www.psychologytoday.com/blog/smart-relationships/201403/affirmations-the-why-what- how-and-what-if

Low, N., S. Butt, P. Ellis, and J. Davis Smith. "Helping out: a national survey of volunteering and charitable giving." London: Cabinet Office, City University of London. Accessed February 2017. http://openaccess.city.ac.uk/2547/

Lyubomirsky, Sonja. "Why are some people happier than others? The role of cognitive and motivational processes in well-being." *American Psychologist* 56, no. 3 (2001): 239-249. Accessed February 2017. http://psycnet.apa.org/doiLanding?doi=10.1037%2F0003-066X.56.3.239

Lyubomirsky, Sonja, Rene Dickerhoof, Julia K. Boehm, and Kennon M. Sheldon. "Becoming Happier Takes Both a Will and a Proper Way: An Experimental Longitudinal Intervention to Boost Well-Being." *Emotion* 11, no. 2 (2011): 391-402.

Martin, Lauren. "The Science Behind Nostalgia and Why We're So Obsessed with the Past." Elite Daily. Accessed December 2016. https://www.elitedaily.com/life/science-behind-nostalgia-love-much/673184

MindTools. "Contingency Planning: Developing a Good 'Plan B'." Accessed November 2017. https://www.mindtools.com/pages/article/newLDR_51.htm

Moll, Jorge, Frank Krueger, Roland Zahn, Matteo Pardini, Ricardo de Oliveira-Souza, and Jordan Grafman. "Human fronto–mesolimbic networks guide decisions about charitable donation." PNAS. Accessed November 2017. https://doi.org/10.1073/pnas.0604475103

Monson, Candice M., Paula P.Schnurr, Patricia A. Resick, Matthew J. Friedman, Young-Xu, Yinong, and Susan P. Stevens. "Cognitive Processing Therapy for Veterans with Military-Related Posttraumatic Stress Disorder." *Journal of Consulting and Clinical Psychology* 74, no. 5 (2006): 898-907.

Morin, Amy. "7 Scientifically Proven Benefits Of Gratitude That Will Motivate You To Give Thanks Year-Round." Forbes. Accessed May 2018. https://www.forbes.com/sites/amymorin/2014/11/23/7-scientifically-proven-benefits-of-gratitude-that-will-motivate-you-to-give-thanks-year-round/#6373591183c0

Moskowitz, Clara. "Mind's Limit Found: 4 Things at Once." Live Science. Accessed November 2017. https://www.livescience.com/2493-mind-limit-4.html

Musolini, Ethan. "Focus on a Few Things." Daily Monitor. Accessed November 2017. http://www.monitor.co.ug/artsculture/Reviews/Focus-on-a-few-things/691232-2787592-7rjpg1z/index.html

Mr. Self-Development. "10 Powerful Prosperity Lessons from Napoleon Hill." Accessed March 2017. http://www.

mrselfdevelopment.com/2010/08/10-powerful-prosperity-lessons-from-napoleon-hill/

Oppong, Thomas. "You Need Clarity of Purpose to Succeed." Medium. Accessed March 2018. https://medium.com/the-mission/you-need-clarity-of-purpose-to-succeed-57a49d061f77

Pareek, Shreya. "This Retired Railway Employee has used his Pension to fill more than 1100 Potholes in Hyderabad." The Better India. Accessed November 2017. https://www.thebetterindia.com/24115/67-year-old-man-used-his-pension-to-fill-dangerous-potholes-of-hyderabad-roads/

Petersen, Neil. "Having a Sense of Purpose in Life Improves Cognition, Mental Health." AllPsych. Accessed June 2016. https://blog.allpsych.com/having-a-sense-of-purpose-in-life-improves-cognition-mental-health/

Post, Stephen G. "Altruism, happiness, and health: it's good to be good." *International Journal of Behavioral Medicine* 12, no. 2 (2005): 66.

Post, Stephen G. *Unlimited Love.* West Conshohocken, PA: Templeton Press, 2003.

Post, Stephen and Jill Neimark. *Why Good Things Happen to Good People: How to Live a Longer, Healthier, Happier Life by the Simple Act of Giving.* New York: Three Rivers Press, 2007.

Poulin, Michael J., Stephanie L. Brown, Amanda J. Dillard, and Dylan M. Smith. "Giving to Others and the Association Between Stress and Mortality." AJPH. Accessed December 2017. http://ajph.aphapublications.org/doi/abs/10.2105/AJPH.2012.300876

Rea, Shilo. "Carnegie Mellon Research Shows Self-Affirmation Improves Problem-Solving Under Stress." Carnegie Mellon University. Accessed November 2017. https://www.cmu.edu/news/stories/archives/2013/may/may3_selfaffirmation.html

Roth, Bernard. *The Achievement Habit: Stop Wishing, Start Doing, and Take Command of Your Life.* New York: Harper Collins, 2015.

Scott, S.J. "30 Awesome Goal Setting Affirmations (How to Stop Procrastinating and Get Things Done.)." Developing Good Habits. Accessed November 2017. https://www.developgoodhabits.com/about-s-j-scott/

Simmons, Steve and John C. Simmons. *Measuring Emotional Intelligence.* New York: Summit Publishing Group, 1997.

Sneed, Rodlescia S. and Sheldon Cohen. "Prospective Study of Volunteerism and Hypertension Risk in Older Adults." *PMC: US National Library of Medicine* 28, no.2 (2013): 578–586.

Tan, Marcus. "What Are the Benefits of Using Positive Affirmation?" Selfgrowth.com Accessed November 2017. http://www.selfgrowth.com/articles/What_Are_The_Benefits_Of_Using_Positive_Affirmation.html

Telis, Gisela. "Multitasking Splits the Brain." Science. Accessed November 2017. http://www.sciencemag.org/news/2010/04/multitasking-splits-brain

Twisted Sifter. "These 10 People Made the World a Better Place. More People Should Know their Names." Accessed December 2017. http://twistedsifter.com/2013/12/10-people-who-made-the-world-a-better-place/

University of Wisconsin-Madison. "Virtue rewarded: Helping others at work makes people happier." Accessed March 2018. https://news.wisc.edu/virtue-rewarded-helping-others-at-work-makes-people-happier/

Vaughan, Michael. "Know Your Limits, Your Brain Can Only Take So Much." Entrepreneur. Accessed December 2017. https://www.entrepreneur.com/article/230925

Wanderlust Worker. "The Harvard MBA Business School Study on Goal Setting." Accessed February 2018. https://www.wanderlustworker.com/the-harvard-mba-business-school-study-on-goal-setting/

Warrell, Margie. *Brave: 50 Everyday Acts of Courage to Thrive in Work, Love and Life.* Hoboken, NJ: John Wiley & Sons, 2015.

Wikipedia. "The Magical Number Seven, Plus or Minus Two." Accessed January 2017. https://en.wikipedia.org/wiki/The_Magical_Number_Seven,_Plus_or_Minus_Two

Zeigler-Hill, Virgil and Todd K. Shackelford. *The SAGE Handbook of Personality and Individual Differences: Volume II: Origins of Personality and Individual Differences.* Thousand Oaks, CA: Sage Publications, 2018.

Ziegler, Erin Holaday. "Gratitude as an Antidote to Aggression." University of Kentucky College of Arts & Sciences. Accessed May 2018. https://psychology.as.uky.edu/gratitude-antidote-aggression

ACKNOWLEDGMENTS

This book is dedicated to my brother Todd. We wrote this book together, and his Spirit is still inspiring me to live on purpose. His life taught me how to laugh hysterically at the irony of life, and his legacy is proof of what it truly means to #goDo and #doGood with an illuminated heart and an ignited soul.

To my parents, Terrence Geary and Beth Isern: Thank you for inspiring an unforgettable life. Your faith in me and your love has led to a life of gratitude. Thank you for all you have taught me about character and how to believe in myself. Nobody thanks their parents enough, but I hope this book is a start.

Thank you to my entire family and especially my sister, Erika Diaz, for reminding me every day that I am perfect exactly as I am. You have filled me with gratitude for family, and helped me to celebrate all of life's little victories. You are a force for good, and I have no clue what our family would do without you!

Paul Bloomberg, thank you for being my best friend and mentor for nearly three decades—that trip to Spain sealed the deal! Your drive and pursuit of making a difference inspires me to wake up every day and craft a better version of myself. Because of you, I'm constantly reminded that *what's for you, won't go by you*. It never has.

An enormous thank you to my creative partner and one of my favorite humans alive: Dr. Wendy Ochoa. You are still one of the few people who can engage my left and right brain while forcing me to search deep inside my heart. I don't say it enough, but thank you.

Tony Francoeur, thank you for teaching me how to #goDo my feelings and what it looks like to #doGood on a daily basis. You inspire authenticity, and remind me that it is OK to allow myself a day to sleep in.

Mary Buckheit, thank you for selecting "Go Do" by Jonsi. The song changed my life. You may never know how much that song has meant to me since the day you decided to add it to our *Summer Mixtape*. Like you, the song has forever changed my life—it might have even saved it.

A special thank you to Tony Robbins and his wife, Bonnie Pearl. The two of you have changed my life in ways I will never be able to communicate in words. The grace you walk this earth with, and the millions of ways you #goDo and #doGood for others, are an absolute inspiration. Because of you, I live more days of my life on purpose (and in more beautiful states).

There are so many brothers and sisters who have been with me throughout the years. Many of you have been silently implied or celebrated throughout these pages, and others need to be thanked personally for all that you have given and taught me.

Jacqueline Delaney, thank you for your friendship and for going on this journey of life with me—every opportunity to see the world with you has been an exercise of living on purpose. And your laugh, it can fill a room!

Kim and Jan, you've added so much meaning to the word "family," and I'm blessed that our paths continue to cross on this walk of life. I love you. I love you. I love you.

Carolann Dekker, thank you for being a member of my "cabinet", a mentor, friend, and a guiding light. To this day, I'm always grateful for each opportunity I get to share a space with you, learn from you, and explore more of New York City with you.

Ryan Espinosa, meeting you was nothing short of a miracle. I'm grateful that our purpose in life was aligned and has given us the gift to support one another's passion to pursue living on purpose.

Thank you Kyla Asbell, Megan Hearne, Jan Phillips, Natalie Susi, Lorraine Tegeris, Brooke van Cleve, and Lily Anna Wanja for all that you put into making sure this book is something the world can #goDo and #doGood with.

Thank you to my publishing team— Jenn T. Grace, Niki

Garcia, Karen Ang, and the entire team at *Publish Your Purpose Press*. No matter how many times I sent this book back with new chapters and more text, you gracefully turned it into a masterpiece.

A deeply heartfelt *thank you* to every person I have ever had the privilege of sharing my life with. Those experiences serve as the defining moments of my being—the transformative crucibles that led to me writing this book, and the human evolution that opened my heart. In my mind, you will always be the change makers of my life—you have shown me the power of #goLaughing, #goLiving, #goGiving, and #goDoing. My time with you still ignites my passion to #doGood for others each day I'm given the gift of life. Each of you has been an invaluable lesson to me on this journey. For that, I thank you.

Finally, I want to acknowledge the world's aspiring leaders, activists, and those fighting for equality and human dignity. You are people of all ages, races, nationalities, sexual orientations, and other diverse backgrounds who wake up each day and #goDo and #doGood in the face of fear, doubt, and uncertainty. I know you possess a fire in you that makes the world turn, but when you fall tired, remember that you can #goDo anything. Keep #goDoing. The world will always hold a space for another #goDoer and #doGooder.

Ask me how I know.

Now let's #goDo together!

ABOUT THE AUTHOR

Talonya Geary, author of *#goDo: How to Live on Purpose*, is a social entrepreneur, consultant, and highly sought-after speaker with over 20 years of experience in business and talent development. Her passion for community visibility, equality, growth, and contribution inspired her to create FlawLes Media and FlawLes Magazine—serving as co-founder and Chief Eternal Optimist—as well as forming Suite T Consulting, Inc. and working as its Principal Consultant and keynote speaker.

Over the last decade, Talonya has brought her unique gifts to the personal and professional development arena, working with some of the world's top thought leaders and influencers, including Tony Robbins.

Today she serves as co-founder and CEO of Spiire, a leading-edge talent development firm in New York City dedicated to unleashing human potential through authenticity, inclusion, and innovation. She is an experienced consultant for young and seasoned professionals, and helps move corporations forward with transformational learning experiences in a variety of key development areas, working with them to quickly create organizational shifts that grow human, social, intellectual, and financial capital.

When she's not traveling the world, Talonya supports non-profit organizations and initiatives to activate resources that benefit underprivileged women and children, and to increase visibility and equality for the LGBTQ community.

Find out more at
TalonyaGeary.com

Made in the USA
San Bernardino, CA
09 October 2018